THE UKRAINIAN INSURGENT ARMY (UPA)

By

Oleh Martowych

UKRAINIAN INFORMATION SERVICE
München 8, Zeppelinstr. 67

The Naval & Military Press Ltd

Published by

The Naval & Military Press Ltd
Unit 10 Ridgewood Industrial Park,
Uckfield, East Sussex,
TN22 5QE England

Tel: +44 (0) 1825 749494
Fax: +44 (0) 1825 765701

www.naval-military-press.com
www.military-genealogy.com
www.militarymaproom.com

In reprinting in facsimile from the original, any imperfections are inevitably reproduced and the quality may fall short of modern type and cartographic standards.

THE UKRAINIAN INSURGENT ARMY

By

OLEH MARTOWYCH

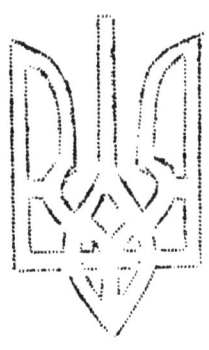

U K R A I N I A N   I N F O R M A T I O N   S E R V I C E

München 8, Zeppelinstr. 67

1950

> "OUR CAUSE IS THE CAUSE OF ALL
> MANKIND, AND WE ARE FIGHTING FOR
> THEIR LIBERTY IN DEFENDING OUR
> OWN"
>
> Benjamin Franklin, 1777

THE ANTI SOVIET RESISTANCE MOVEMENT OF THE UKRAINIAN PEOPLE ON NATIVE SOIL

ITS HISTORY   ITS GROWTH
ITS STATUS AT PRESENT

Table of Contents

	Page
Chapter I Introduction to the Ukrainian Problem	1
Chapter II The Struggle for the Liberation of Ukraine	2
Chapter III The Standard Technique of Bolshevizing a Nation	2
Chapter IV The Ukrainian Resistance Movement between the Two Wars (1921-1941)	4
Chapter V The Ukrainian Resistance Movement versus German Nazism (1941-1944)	10
Chapter VI The Ukrainian Resistance Movement versus the Kremlin (1944-1949)	20
Chapter VII Ukrainians in their Struggle for Freedom	44
Chapter VIII The Political Program of the Ukrainian Resistance Movement	49
Chapter IX The Territory of Ukraine under the Control of the Ukrainian Resistance Movement	52
Chapter X The Forces of the Ukrainian Resistance Movement and their Organization	54
Chapter XI The Soviet Methods of Combatting the Ukrainian Resistance Movement	60
Chapter XII The Ukrainian Resistance Movement and the Western Powers	74

1. Introduction to Ukrainian Problem

The Ukrainian problem, one of the most complicated in the whole of modern Europe, is superbly simple if the idea is once accepted that the Ukrainians are a _separate_ people, distinct from the Russians.

Nationally, the USSR is not a homogenous entity, as many "specialists" on East European affairs would lead the world to believe but a diverse multiplicity of races and peoples subjugated by Moscow. Thus, Ukraine is nationally and culturally a distinct and a separate nation, the most easterly stronghold of western civilization in Eastern Europe. Modern research in the anthropology and archeology of Eastern Europe makes it plain that these two distinct national ethnic types, the Russian and Ukrainian, existed long before the Tartar invasions of Eastern Europe in the 13th century. The Ukrainian language, which is quite different from the Russian, the Ukrainian manners and customs, national art, and historical traditions, all these are external characteristics which distinctly set the Ukrainian people apart from the Russians. But the deepest cleavage between the two peoples is found in Ukrainian mentality and idealism, which are completely at variance with the mentality of the Russians. A Ukrainian is an individualist and a Russian exactly the opposite. By nature, the Ukrainians are true democrats and opponents of all forms of dictatorship and tyranny. The contrary is true of the Russians, who have a natural inclination to accept an absolute government imposed by force and remain subservient to it. As William C. Bullitt writes in his "The Great Globe Itself": "From the time of the Mongols until today, the Russians have been inured to living in a totalitarian state under the tyranny of an absolute dictator" (p.28). And Soviet dictatorship is typical of the same barbaric despotism as the autocracies of Ivan the Terrible, Peter I, Catherine II, and the like.

Here the Ukrainians, in contrast to the Russians, are decidedly western in outlook. They always regarded themselves as independent and free citizens and they place the highest value on freedom, to which they are devoted whole-heartedly. Ukraine was territory which was impregnated with all the cultural movements of Western Europe. The crusaders, the Magdeburg Law, humanism, the Reformation, baroque, penetrated to Ukraine and were analogous to the trends in the West. The culture of the French Enlightenment became the source of the national regeneration of Ukraine in the 19th century. Likewise, contemporary Ukrainian seeks inspiration in the creative culture of western Europe, whereas Russia has evolved its own way of life, its own world, hostile to the West.

In the spring of 1945, the Ukrainian Soviet Socialist Republic was formally accepted at the Conference in San Francisco as a member of the United Nations Organization. This could not satisfy the aspirations of the forty million Ukrainians suffering under the Communist yoke, but it did bring prominently before the public opinion of the world the fact that Ukraine is not the creation of propagandists, not a "German intrigue" but a nation with its own geographical areas, its own population and its own history.

2. The Struggle for the Liberation of Ukraine

The history of Ukraine throughout the ages is a tragic story of a great people who have been doomed to suffer for six hundred years every form of oppression that the mind of man can create. With it all, the Ukrainians have clung to their own land, language and traditions. Every time there has been an upheaval in Europe, the Ukrainians have responded to it and have sought to secure the right to determine their own national destiny.

The present struggle of the UPA (Ukrainian Insurgent Army) is a continuation of that centuries-old struggle which the Ukrainian people have been waging to win their national freedom. The independence of Ukraine and the union of all Ukrainian lands into ONE NATIONAL STATE has been the ideal of the Ukrainian people for centuries. This ideal has its origin in the national memory of the independence and feeling of fraternal unity, enjoyed during the periods of the great and progressive Ukrainian Kievan State of Volodymyr the Great (981-1015) and Yaroslav the Wise (1018-1054). This ideal was the acme in the careers of the Ukrainian Cromwell, Bohdan Khmelnitsky (1648-1657) and the great patriot Ivan Mazeppa (1686-1709) and it almost saw its realization at time of World War I (1914-1918).

In the period between the First and Second World Wars, the struggle of the Ukrainians for the liberation did not cease, - it merely went through different phases depending upon existing circumstances. World War II created favourable circumstances for the strengthening of the Ukrainian struggle for liberation. Manifesting its aspirations for freedom under the German occupation, the Ukrainian Resistance Movement created its armed resistance groups in 1942 and by 1943 those were united into a big and powerful Ukrainian Insurgent Army (UPA) under one supreme command. Through its strategical and political activities the Ukrainian Insurgent Army (UPA) supported by the entire Ukrainian people, greatly contributed to the destruction of the German armed forces in Ukraine.

When the Soviet forces reoccupied Ukraine the Ukrainian Resistance Movement with its Ukrainian Insurgent Army (UPA) met them fully prepared for the political and military struggle. For this struggle it mobilized not only hundreds of thousands of Ukrainians but also other peoples whose countries were subjugated by the Bolshevists. Today the struggle for the liberation of Ukraine continues unabated and thus, the Ukrainian Insurgent Army (UPA) has entered into its 7th year of existence. It has been proudly offering stern opposition to the powerful Soviet Union, whose excellently trained detachments of the MGB (GPU=NKVD=NKGB=MGB=Soviet political police) are not quite capable of coping with it. This struggle spreading from Ukraine to other countries has recently received great publicity throughout the world.

3. The Standard Technique of Bolshevizing a Nation

At the close of World War I, and especially after the fall of the Tsarist Russian prison of peoples, the Ukrainians proclaimed the Ukrainian Independent State on January 22, 1918. This proclamation was the expression of the will of the whole Ukrainian people. The reborn Ukrainian state had a democratic-socialist government and its first President was the famous Ukrainian historian and archaeologist, Prof. Michael Hrushevsky. For a while it seemed as if a final solution of the future of

Ukraine had been reached.

But then for the first time, the standard technique of bolshevizing a nation was adopted in Ukraine. The same technique was later used in many other countries, e.g. 1920 in Armenia and Azerbaijan, 1921 in Georgia, 1923 in the Far East Republic and in Outer Mongolia, 1939-1940 in Western Ukraine and Western Byelorussia, Estonia, Latvia and Lithuania, 1944-1946 in Bulgaria, Yugoslavia, Albania, Rumania, Hungary, Czechoslovakia, Poland, Eastern Germany, Northern Korea etc. The action against Ukraine was then directed by the Russian Commissar of Nationalities, Joseph Stalin. He induced the Executive Committee of the local Kyiv Soviet Council of Peasants, Workers, and Soldiers to call an All-Ukrainian Convention of Soviets. This was to precede the elections for the Ukrainian Constituent Assembly in order to produce a <u>coup d'état</u>, to overthrow the Ukrainian democratic government and to proclaim the government of the Soviets in Ukraine. But this meeting proved clearly that Bolshevism in Ukraine was a foreign intrigue of the Russian government against the independence of Ukraine. Of the 2 000 only 150 delegates (and the majority of them were non-Ukrainians) took a stand against the Ukrainian government. The over-whelming majority proclaimed their full loyalty to the Ukrainian government and the meeting became an enthusiastic demonstration for the independence of Ukraine.

The small minority of the Ukrainian Soviets Conference, some 150 delegates, only about 7,5% of the total number attending it, led by the Russian Sergiev (Artem) left Kyiv and moved to Kharkiv on the border of Red Russia, and there opened their own conference of Soviets and proclaimed Ukraine a Soviet Republic. They named themselves the Soviet Government of Ukraine and applied to the Russian Soviet Government for aid.

In order to sovietize Ukraine the Red Army marched in, and the Ukrainian War of Independence (1918-1921) began. The defensive war of Ukraine lasted <u>four</u> years and the Ukrainian Army was compelled to conduct an unequal struggle against the Red and White Russians, Poles and Rumanians. As the result of the numerical superiority of the enemies' forces, the Ukrainian Independent State fell, after years of desperate fighting. Ukraine was conquered by the Bolshevists and became the Ukrainian Soviet Socialist Republic. Western Ukraine was divided among Poland (Galicia and Volhynia), Rumania (northern Bukovina and Bessarabia) and Czechoslovakia (Carpatho-Ukraine).

For the Ukrainians there is little consolation in the fact that they saved Europe by their prolonged resistance against the Bolshevists in this war, because they themselves fell victims of the most ruthless oppression under the Soviet regime. Unfortunately, the Ukrainian fight for freedom had found no sympathetic understanding throughout the democratic world. Attempts to obtain consideration for the claims of Ukrainian independence abroad were not successful. There was little knowledge of the historical side of the Ukrainian question among the representatives of the leading powers. France was committed to the idea of a "strong Poland", the United States was comparatively un-interested in eastern Europe and Great Britain wavered between the aggressively anti-Bolshevik policy of Winston Churchill, then Secretary of War, who aided the Russian White leaders (Kolchak and Denikin) with arms, munitions and supplies and the impulses of Prime Minister

Lloyd George to seek a basis of agreement with the Soviet regime. Instead of aiding the Ukrainians in their fight against the Bolshevists, the Allies had decided to back Denikin, the enemy of Ukraine, who simultaneously fought the Ukrainians, using the British war materials. This devious policy caused failure to establish a stable government in Ukraine, led to anarchy, and asphyxiated the Ukrainian Army by a terrible blockade. Even food and medical supplies were not allowed to enter the territory occupied by the Ukrainian Army. The artificially created typhus epidemic took the lives of thousands of Ukrainian soldiers and civilians because of the lack of medicines and injections.

The Ukrainians are fully conscious of the fact that if they had received the support the Russian White leaders did from Great Britain and France, they would never have succumbed and Bolshevism would not have overrun Ukraine and Europe. The World War II would never have taken place, as the Ribbentrop-Molotov agreement, which was the starting signal for this war, could not be concluded because of lack of partners. Thus, the devious policy followed by the Allies caused the subjugation of Ukraine by Moscow and then the sovietization of the nation.

The standard technique of bolshevizing a nation was well illustrated in Europe after the Soviet "victory" of 1945. Ukraine was the first country in the world to experience it. Here, in order to sovietize a population, it was necessary to deport thousands of nationally conscious Ukrainians to vast concentration camps in Russia, chiefly in Siberia. All of the educated classes, the teachers, clergymen, professional and business-men, well-to-do farmers and democratic leaders were removed by force. Millions of the population perished in famines artificially created to break their spirit. Those of the cultural leaders who remained loyal to their belief and their traditions were executed or died by their own hand (Mykola Khvylovy) to escape a worse fate. Everything was done to eat out the heart of the Ukrainian spirit and to give it a Russian Communist aspect. But the Bolshevists did not succeed in breaking the Ukrainian national spirit. This fact is well known among the well-informed. Stalin, a realist, is well acquainted with the dynamic qualities of the centuries-old Ukrainian national movement. Back in 1934, at the XVIIth Congress of the Communist Party, he warned against it and called Ukrainian nationalism a "grave danger" for the Soviet Union. Today, his lieutenant in Ukraine, Khrushchev, has repeatedly given similar statements and has called for constant vigilance against "Ukrainian bourgeois nationalism". Ukrainian nationalism is a very concrete factor in eastern European affairs - and on more than one occasion stirred up trouble for the Kremlin.

4. Ukrainian Resistance Movement between the Two Wars (1921-1941)

The national spirit of the Ukrainians did not die. Military defeat of the Ukrainian armies in the War of Independence did not weaken the struggle for the liberation of the Ukrainian nation. The Ukrainian War of Independence has an immense importance for the formation of the Ukrainian national ideal. The independence of Ukraine as well as the unity of all Ukrainian lands proclaimed during that war became the BASIC DOGMA OF POLITICAL FAITH OF THE UKRAINIAN PEOPLE. During the period from that time to the present, millions of Ukrainians have sacrificed their lives for the realization of this ideal and have manifested to the whole world that the Ukrainians have a supreme desire to be A FREE AND UNITED

NATION in Europe.

Several years after the War of Independence, many Ukrainian, armed groups of partisans were active against the Soviet regime and eventually were transformed into an underground political organization resisting the Soviets. There were also attempts to oppose the Soviet regime by such means as opposition within the Communist Party of Ukraine and the Ukrainian Soviet government. Two representatives of this tendency in the twenties were O. Shumsky, who was for a time Commissar for Education, and M. Volobuyev, famous journalist and economist. Shumsky rose up in defence of the Ukrainian national position in the Communist Party and tried to take advantage of the cultural Ukrainization ordered by the Communist Party to strengthen the Ukrainian national spirit (1926). Volobuyev exposed in his articles the "colonization tendencies of Soviet economic policy in Ukraine" (1928).

Another rebel among the Ukrainian Communists was the popular writer Mykola Khvylovy. He vindicated the right of Ukraine to maintain cultural contacts with the West - as an indirect form of resisting domination from Moscow. The Russian Communists regarded Khvylovy and his friends as Ukrainian nationalists. Moscow became truly alarmed when Khvylovy issued his "Literary Manifesto" in which he called upon the Ukrainian writers not to imitate Russian literary trends and not to seek inspiration in Russian culture because, as he said, "it lacked healthy elements". Instead, he recommended "to turn the backs to Moscow and the faces to Western Europe". As early as 1929 Stalin himself made the following reference to Khvylovy: "If we had nothing else but these discussions about Khvylovy, which have become so wide and heated in Ukraine, there would be sufficient cause for profound alarm." Khvylovy committed suicide in May, 1933, probably because he foresaw arrest and execution as a nationalist.

The attack of the Communist Party and its agencies on Ukrainian culture began in the early thirties and grew to tremendous dimensions. Between 1933 and 1934, and between 1936 and 1938 huge purges took place which were especially felt by the Ukrainian intellectuels, men of science and culture who opposed Soviet attempts to destroy Ukrainian national culture and to supplant it with a Russianized communist culture alien to the spirit and soul of the Ukrainian people. In these years the Bolshevists annihilated scholars, writers, artists, military men, political leaders and thousands and tens of thousands of thinking people who formed its highest stratum. Among all these tortured leaders of Ukrainian art, literature and science, there were many great names and men of undoubted talents, known and honored not only in Ukraine, but throughout the world (e.g. Prof. Michael Hrushevsky, famous historian and archaelogist, or Prof. Stepan Rudnytsky, famous geographer, etc.). Among seventy-nine authors and scientists, executed by Soviet firing squads in December, 1934, were such talented Ukrainians as Hryhory Kosynko, Kost Buroviy, Oleksa Vlyzko, Dmytro Falkivsky and others. Many others were exiled: Mykola Kulish, the great Ukrainian dramatist, Valerian Pidmohylny, Borys Antonenko-Davydovych, Volodymyr Gzhytsky - the well-known novelists, Mykola Zerov - the poet and professor of Ukrainian literature at the University of Kyiv, Pavlo Filipovich, Mykhaylo Dray-Khmara, Evhen Pluzhnyk - the poets, Ostap Vyshnya - very popular satirist. Thus perished many scientists - professors such as Yefremiv, Doroshkevych, Slabchenko, Hantsov, the artists Padalka, Boychuk, Les Kurbas, army officers Tyutyunnyk, Dubovy.

The Ukrainian peasantry strongly opposed the economic policy of the Soviet government, as exemplified by its forced collectivization of Ukrainian agriculture. The peasants had been as turbulent in Ukraine as anywhere else in rebelling against the forced Stalinite collectivization. Crushed by the famine created artificially for political purposes in 1932/33 they gave up the struggle for individual landholdings and entered the collective farms. It seems clear that at least ten per cent of the population of Ukraine starved to death during this famine. There has probably been in history no disaster of comparable magnitude that received so little international attention.

After the period of mass anti-Bolshevik risings in Ukraine (1921-1924) the Ukrainian Resistance Movement assumed the form of secret political organizations. In 1930 an organization called "Union for the Liberation of Ukraine" was discovered in Ukraine and a group of alleged members were brought to trial. Forty-five Ukrainian intellectuals were tried in Kharkiv (1930), and all were condemned to slave labor, including Serhiy Yefremiv, Vice-President of the Academy of Sciences, Volodymyr Chekhivsky, head of the Ukrainian Autocephalic Orthodox Church, Andrew Nikovsky, former Minister of the Ukrainian National Republic, and others. The same year witnessed the discovery of S.U.M. (Union of the Ukrainian Youth) and some 20,000 of alleged members of this organization were executed in Ukraine. In 1931 the discovery of a Ukrainian organization known as the "Nationalist Centre" was announced, and in connection with this a number of political leaders who had formerly been associated with the Ukrainian democratic government, including Holubovich, Shershel and Mazurenko were executed. In 1933 the ever-active G.P.U. announced the discovery of a Ukrainian Military Organization (U.V.O.) and among the prominent individuals who were shot in connection with this case was Yuri Kotsiubinsky, the former Vice-President of the Council of People's Commissars. The same year, 1933, witnessed the suicide of the veteran Ukrainian Communist, Lenin's friend, Mykola Skrypnyk, who was Vice-President of the Council of People's Commissars and acting Commissar for Education. In 1934, another "nationalist organization" was discovered and in connection with the assassination of Kirov many prominent Ukrainians were shot in retaliation.

During the next few years the purges continued. For reasons which can never be fully clarified, the men who showed the greatest energy in stamping out Ukrainian nationalism often fell victims to the purge themselves. This was the case with Postishev, Stalin's principal lieutenant in Ukraine in the thirties, with Kosior, who at the same time occupied the post of Secretary of the Communist Party in Ukraine. In 1937, Moscow sent to Ukraine Lazar Kaganovich with the purpose of liquidating the Ukrainian opposition. Under his pressure another prominent Ukrainian Communist, Panas Lubchenko, President of the Council of the People's Commissars of Ukraine, after boasting once that Ukrainian nationalism had been eliminated by the firm policy of the Communist Party, was apparently suspected of nationalism himself and committed suicide rather than face a trial in which the result was a foregone conclusion. Still another Prime Minister, Bondarenko, vanished mysteriously from the political scene and is presumably dead or in exile. Thus all Prime Ministers of the Ukrainian SSR from Rakovsky to Bondarenko were liquidated by the Soviets.

Still another important current in the Ukrainian nationalist movement was represented by the O.U.N. (Organization of Ukrainian Nationalists). It emerged from the U.V.O. (Ukrainian Military Organization) and accepted a regular plan of action based on firm ideological foundations aiming at the political, spiritual and social liberation of the Ukrainian people from foreign misrule. The O.U.N. was strongly disciplined revolutionary anti-Soviet and anti-Polish force which created a number of illegal groups armed as far as possible. The leading figure in the O.U.N. and perhaps the most militant figure in the Ukrainian nationalist movement after the murder of Gen. Simon Petlura in Paris (1926) was Col. Evhen Konovalets. He met his death when a Soviet agent in a cafe in Rotterdam handed him a bomb which exploded killing him (1938).

The Ukrainian reaction to Polish rule in Western Ukraine took other forms. Historically the relation between the Pole and the Ukrainian had never been cordial. The proclamation of the Republic of Western Ukraine on November 1, 1918 and the resulting Polish-Ukrainian war in Eastern Galicia only increased the bitterness which had been developed by history. From the first days of the existence of the Republic of Western Ukraine the Ukrainians had to defend themselves against Poland and Rumania. The Soviet aggression against Eastern Ukraine was really leaving Western Ukraine to itself and by the summer of 1919 Polish military control had been extended over the whole of Western Ukraine. The 100.000 men strong Ukrainian Galician Army passed into Eastern Ukraine and joined the Ukrainian forces under Gen. Simon Petlura's command which fought against the Bolshevist invaders. The brilliant offensive of the combined Ukrainian forces against the Bolshevists caused the total defeat of the Bolshevist forces in Ukraine and led to the seizure of the Ukrainian capital - Kyiv, on Aug. 31, 1919 where the Ukrainian armies were insidiously attacked by the advancing White-Russian army of Gen. Denikin.

The Allied Supreme Council on June 25, 1919 authorized the Poles to occupy Eastern Galicia up to the line of the river Zbruch, the old frontier between Austria-Hungary and Russia. Finally the Treaty of Riga, 1921, secured from the Soviet-Union the recognition of the Polish control over the Western Ukraine. For a time the Allied powers refused to recognize the Polish occupation of Western Ukraine, but there was no desire to challenge it by armed force. The situation was complicated and the Polish Parliament passed a law in the autumn 1922, establishing autonomy for Eastern Galicia. This paved the way for the recognition of Poland's possession of Eastern Galicia by the Conference of Ambassadors on March 14, 1923 over the articulate protests of the Ukrainian people. Unfortunately steps were never taken to fulfill the unilateral promises contained in the autonomy law of September, 1922, and Eastern Galicia was always governed from Warsaw.

From year to year the Ukrainian Resistance Movement in Poland changed its form as various measures were put into effect by the Polish government to break down the Ukrainians. The legal opposition represented by the legal political parties (the Ukrainian National-Democratic Union, the Ukrainian Radical-Socialist Party, and the Ukrainian Socialist-Democratic Party) advocated the policy of obtaining maximum rights for the Ukrainians within the

Polish state, and at the same time stressed the right of all Ukrainians to unite themselves in a sovereign and democratic Ukraine within Ukrainian ethnographic boundaries. The clandestine opposition represented by the U.V.O. (Ukrainian Military Organisation) and by the O.U.N. (Organization of Ukrainian Nationalists), organized surprise attacks on individual Polish officials who were held responsible for oppressive acts of the Government. Such an attack was the assassination of the Polish Minister of Interior P i e r a c k i in Warsaw, 1934. He was responsible for the "pacification" of the Ukrainians in the fall of 1930. This "pacification", as it was officially and euphomistically termed, was quite widely reported in the American press at that time. After the statement of Minister Pieracki that "the Ukrainians must be burned out with white-hot steel, and for every act of Ukrainian revolutionary organizations, Poland must continue to punish the entire population upon the principle of collective responsibility", brutal reprisals were inflicted relatively indiscriminately on the Ukrainian population by Polish troops and police. Libraries and co-operatives were destroyed, Boy Scout organizations were dissolved, Ukrainian high schools and institutions of every kind were closed, and concentration camps were established. Several thousand Ukrainians were in prisons or in camps, and the majority of arrested Ukrainians remained in jail for a long time without any charge being preferred against them, while the police hunted for evidence.

The cultural and economic methods of suppression were demonstrated in the Polish campaign to abolish Ukrainian schools, churches, co-operatives and cultural and sports organizations. For example, the Ukrainian Encyclopedia estimated that there were only 134 Ukrainian schools left in Western Ukraine in 1930. In 1924 there were 2,417 and under Austria-Hungary there were 3,414 primary schools. In the Summer of 1938 alone, the Polish government destroyed at least 112 Orthodox churches belonging to Ukrainians, on the pretext that they had once been Uniate (i.e. united with Rome, Catholic of Eastern Rite). Such an act, which drew the protest of the Greek-Catholic Metropolitan of Lviv Magr. Count Sheptitsky, only succeeded in antagonizing both the Uniates (Greek-Catholics) and the Orthodox against the Poles and in bringing the two religious groups closer together.

The "Service d'Informations Ukrainiennes" of Paris estimated that after 1921, 914 political trials of Ukrainians were held, excluding those of communists, and that 65% were against persons accused of activity in behalf of the U.V.O. and O.U.N. Of a total of 3,777 persons tried, 2510 were found guilty, 17 were sentenced to death, 27 were sentenced to life imprisonment and the others to a total of 5,870 years imprisonment. In 1939 alone, however, the arrests convictions and years of imprisonment meted out surpassed the totals of all those from 1921-1938. For example, in August alone, the month before the Nazi invasion 111 Ukrainians were tried on political charges and 75 were found guilty. These were given sentences totalling 132 1/2 years imprisonment. Most were charged with membership in the O.U.N.

It must not be thought that the Ukrainians have done nothing but revolt. Even during the years of oppression, the Ukrainians continued to solidify their position in the state. They tried to build up a life of their own and created completely managed organizations for assisting education, spreading Ukrainian culture, meliorating agriculture, etc. Their co-operative organizations increased in numbers, in capital and in membership. Thus the number of co-operatives belonging to the Ukrainian Auditing Association at Lviv was only 1029 at the start of 1925 and grew to 3337 by 1934. By 1939 the Ukrainians of the West were in a much better position than they had been before and they constituted a variety of a "state within a state".

The Soviet government always regarded the Ukrainian nationalist movement in Western Ukraine as a dangerous enemy. One of the reasons Stalin has been insistent on annexing Poland's former eastern provinces stems from his desire to bring all the Ukrainians under his rule and stamp out all traces of non-communist Ukrainian nationalism. It is significant that in spite of the constant struggle of the Ukrainians against Polish oppression, the Western Ukrainians remained bitterly and stead-fastly anti-communist and considered themselves champions of Ukrainian independence and unification of all Ukrainian lands into one Ukrainian sovereign state. There was hardly another country in Europe where anti-communist feelings were stronger than in the semi-proletarian Western Ukraine. The suddenly-revealed conclusion of the Ribbentrop-Molotov non-aggression pact on August 23, 1939, rendered possible the realization of Stalin's plans of annexing Western Ukraine. On September 17, 1939, the Soviet Army invaded Western Ukraine despite various treaties with Poland, on the ground that the Polish Republic had ceased to exist as an organized state and occupied the whole of Western Ukraine giving official aim: "liberation" and "protection" of the Ukrainian "brethren". Again Western Ukraine first fell the victim of the Bolshevist imperialism. On June 28, 1940 the Russian Bolshevists "liberated" other parts of Western Ukraine which in 1918-1919 had been seized by Rumanians, e.i. northern Bukovina with its capital Chernivtsi and parts of Bessarabia. These were incorporated into the Ukrainian Soviet Socialist Republic.

We are more than certain that the fate of Eastern Europe could have been much different had the restored Poland and Rumania acted more wisely and with a sense of historical responsibility in regard to Ukraine. Instead of being guided by the political reason, they had apparently fallen under the spell of chauvinistic blindness and under the mania of political greatness. Especially, the newly created Poland, largely supported by the Allies, committed an unpardonable crime by attacking the Ukrainians, who, like Poland itself, after the fall of the Russian and Austro-Hungarian Empires, had sought freedom and independence. This attack was timed with the onslaughts of the Russian Bolsheviks who invaded the Ukrainian National Republic from the north and east. It is already a matter of history how the Poles deceived the Allies by claiming that all help provided was being used against the Russian Bolsheviks, whereas the true fact is that whatever aid the Poles obtained in 1919 was directed against the Ukrainians, or by promising autonomy for the Ukrainians and never carrying it out into effect. The fact is that Poland helped the Russian Bolshevists to establish their control over Ukraine, securing for itself the control over the part of the Ukrainian lands. In consequence when the time of Hitler-Stalin Axis came in being Poland could not resist against the 4th partition of Poland. Poland has lost the Ukrainian lands once and for ever, and, what is more, has lost her own independence and has sunk to the role of a Russian satellite. The Russian Bolsheviks have helped the Ukrainians and Poles to settle their neighbourly accounts and the Kremlin has made up the bill. Such is the sad finale of the old-age Polish-Ukrainian relations and of the Polish blundering policy towards the Ukrainians.

It is interesting to note that the very first opposition to Hitler's plans was offered by the Ukrainian Resistance Movement in Carpatho-Ukraine, a small mountainous country which was a part of Czechoslovakia since 1919. When in the autumn of 1938 Czechoslovakia was rebuilt along federal lines, Carpatho-Ukraine gained autonomy. In March 1939, at the time when Mr. Hacha, president of Czechoslovakia surrendered the freedom of his state, and the Czech army did not fire a single shot in defence of its lands, the freedom-loving Ukrainians, not in the habit of bowing to aggressors, organized bitter armed resistance against the Hungarians and Hitler when Hitler let his puppet Hungarian army march against Carpatho-Ukraine. It was the first shot fired against the so-called Nazi New Order in Europe and this shot was fired by the Ukrainian Resistance Movement. The small country of Carpatho-Ukraine won then the sympathy and admiration of the world.

Nowadays, Carpatho-Ukraine is also a part of the Ukrainian Soviet Socialist Republic. The first president of Carpatho-Ukraine, Msgr. Augustine Boloshyn had been arrested by the Soviets and died in a Soviet prison. Thus, Stalin succeeded in uniting all the Ukrainian lands under his rule.

5. The Ukrainian Resistance Movement versus German Nazism (1941-1944)

Poland was partitioned between the Soviet-Union and Nazi Germany according to the honeymoon Ribbentrop-Molotov pact in the autumn of 1939. Eastern Galicia and Volhynia with their large Ukrainian population were incorporated into the Soviet-Ukraine. Elections were held in Western-Ukraine after the Soviet occupation. In keeping with the usual Communist technique, a "Provisional Popular Assembly" made up of Communists and of individuals who were regarded as politically reliable voted on October 27, 1939, for union with the Soviet Ukraine. By a decree of August 2, 1940, Northern Bukovina and the parts of Bessarabia were also absorbed into the Soviet-Ukraine.

Active Ukrainian resisters remained in the country and worked out plans for the development of the Ukrainian Resistance Movement in the whole of this enlarged Soviet-Ukraine. They succeeded in organizing the cells of the Ukrainian Resistance Movement in Donbas (Donets coal basin) and in all large cities of Ukraine (Dnipropetrovsk, Kharkiv, Odessa). It was possible as many members of the Ukrainian Resistance Movement were transferred there, having volunteered to work in factories and mines of the Ukrainian industrial regions.

When the Germans struck at the Soviet-Union, on June 22, 1941, Ukrainian resistance forces took advantage of the confusion and demoralization in the Soviet occupied regions and seized control of many places (Buchach, Tovmach, etc.).

Three days (from 24-26 of June) a street-fighting was carried on in Lviv, the largest city of Western-Ukraine. The Soviet troops were overtaken by a tremendous panic. Soviet tanks bombarded the churches of this city naively believing them to be the centers of the revolt. On June 27, 1941, Soviet front troops succeeded in restoring order. On this day the NKCD troops massacred the Ukrainians in the prisons of Lviv which were literally filled with the corpses of the murdered Ukrainians. The same scenes were repeated in the cities and towns of Western and Eastern Ukraine, namely in Sambir, Stryj, Stanyslaviv, Zolochiv, Ternopil, Bubno, Lutsk, Rivne, Berdychiv, Zhitomir, Vinnytsia, Dnipropetrovsk,

Kyiv, Poltava, Kharkiv, and many others. In some prisons (Sambir, etc.) the prisoners revolted and succeeded in escaping their fate.

However, on the night of June 30, 1941, the Ukrainian underground forces took possession of the radio-station in Lviv and proclaimed from there the re-establishment of the Ukrainian Independent State (June 30, 1941). This proclamation was a clear challenge to the German government to declare its policy all the more the Germans in their first appeals promised the Ukraine heaven and earth trying to win their favor.

Had the Germans been willing to co-operate with the Ukrainian Resistance Movement in its fight for Ukrainian independence and not to interfere with internal problems of the Ukrainian Independent State, a good deal of Ukrainian-German co-operation might have been expected. The Germans might have won the war in Eastern Europe if they had fully exploited the power of the Ukrainian resistance Movement and other subjugated nations. Ukraine would have been able to raise an army of 3-4 million men and immense resources for this fight.

However, the Germans came not as liberators but as conquerors. They made no effort to consult the wishes of the subjugated peoples of the Soviet-Union and establish the national independent states in Eastern Europe. The Nazi leadership, drunk with power and success, chose to follow a policy of unilateral conquest, domination and enslavement. The Germans did not want allies in Eastern Europe, but slaves. They sought only for "quislings" who would consent as German collaborators to push the people into a definitely subordinate position as a subject race. Long before they lost their war strategically, the Germans lost their war politically. They played the trumpcards in Stalin's hands chiefly by their backward policy in Eastern Europe. Today there is no doubt that the chief reason for Hitler's debacle in the East stemmed from his blundering policy, especially in Ukraine.

The reaction of Gestapo to the Ukrainian proclamation of June 30, 1941, came very swiftly. The Ukrainian government was liquidated and prominent Ukrainian patriots were shot or imprisoned. During the opening weeks of the campaign in the East, Ukrainians deserted from the Soviet armies by hundreds of thousands. They expected to take part in the liberation of their country, but Hitler sent them to the camps to die of hunger and misery. He flatly rejected all plans to draw the Ukrainian people and the peoples of the Soviet territories into the struggle against the Bolsheviks. He ordered seizing several million Ukrainians, both men and women, and had them sent to Germany as slave laborers, in order to prevent a Ukrainian mass movement. And he ordered a systematic pillaging of the countryside for the benefit of his Germany which chronically lacked foodstuffs.

Thus from the first days of the German occupation of Ukraine a relentless struggle began between the German-Nazis and the Ukrainian people. An extremely complicated struggle for freedom began. The Ukrainian Resistance Movement fought simultaneously against the Germans resisting food requisitions and deportations for slave labor in Germany, and against Soviet armed units. Separate guerilla units, formed by the OUN (Organisation of Ukrainian Nationalists), in 1941, everywhere in Ukraine, and particularly in the northern forest regions of Western and Central Ukraine, were all united as early as December, 1942, under one supreme command. Thus, the Ukrainian Insurgent Army (UPA - Ukrainska Povstancha Armia) came into being.

It should be kept in mind that his guerilla warfare against the Germans was launched at the time when the German power was at its peak and when Nazi Germany was celebrating her greatest military victories. Guerilla warfare flared up at a time when in other nations receiving aid from their governments-in-exile and the support of Western Allies, the formation of a guerilla army was merely a disorganized idea. Thus, the Ukrainian people started their fight against the Nazi invaders at a time when corresponding movements in Western Europe had not yet been born (1942). The Ukrainian Insurgent Army (UPA) was, along with the Polish Home Army, one of the first underground armies which operated on a large scale against Nazi Germany. This struggle cost Ukraine hundred thousand casualties and brought it an unbelievable destruction. What was once a land of proud beauty became one of the most desolate places in whole Eastern Europe.

It must be emphasized that the Ukrainian people took an a c t i v e part in the war against the Nazi-Germany. The Ukrainians have definitely helped to destroy the German menace and the history of their fight against the Nazi-Germany repeatedly attests to the will of the Ukrainian people to be governed by themselves, with their own consent and not to endure brutal rule against their consent. The Ukrainians fought Nazi-Germans in the ranks of the Soviet Army (1st, 2nd, 3rd and 4th Ukrainian armies), in the ranks of the French resistance (Ukrainian battailons under Ukrainian command) and in the ranks of the Ukrainian Insurgent Army (UPA). It gave no rest to the German legions. The Ukrainian population, old men, woman and children organized in guerilla warfare, effectively disrupted German commucations, wrecked their supplies, lines and depots and otherwise demonstrated their full support of the UPA. Owing to this action and favorable terrain UPA was able to accomplish a feat impossible for the underground forces in Western Europe, i.e. the clearing of the enemy out of large regions which then became administrated by the government of the Ukrainian Resistance Movement. In the second half of 1943 and in the first half of 1944 the situation in Eastern Europe was such that Germans could only hold on to main roads and larger urban centers and they were unable to occupy the broad expanses of the country. The rest of the territory was controlled by the UPA and administrated by it. The UPA was the only underground army in Eastern Europe, having under arms about 200,000 Ukrainians = men and women, old and young, workers and farmers, intellectuals and clergymen and being equipped with arms seized from the Germans and the Russians. It had numerous supply centers at its disposal as well as training camps and field hospitals, which were well camoflaged and guarded in the mountains, forests and marshlands. The soldiers of the UPA were well-fed and clothed, the wounded nursed. Consequently, Ukrainian and Jewish doctors, pharmacists, nurses, specialists and social workers were taken into the UPA which, thus, became an armed organization of the whole Ukrainian people. Such a guerilla warfare was only possible because it had the whole-hearted approval of the Ukrainian people.

The Nazi-Germans combatted the Ukrainian Resistance Movement and its Ukrainian Insurgent Army (UPA) by launching offensives against it and by an unheard of terror against the Ukrainian population and, especially, against the Ukrainian intellectuals. Three times during the German occupation (April-May, 1943, July-

October, 1943 and February-March, 1944) the Nazi-Germans launched their offensives against the UPA. The entire campaign was fierce and bitter. The Germans used aircraft, artillery and tanks, followed closely by infantry and police units. Several attacks against UPA were repulsed with heavy losses for the enemy. At long last the Nazi offensives were broken and the Germans were defeated. They then limited themselves to the bombardment of the Ukrainian villages and towns and to the murder of the political prisoners and the non-combatant population in the vicinity of the larger towns. On July 24, 1943, three Ukrainian villages Toolychiv, Lityn and Radovych were destroyed by the German police and several hundred defenseless people were murdered. On July 14, 1943 a terrible slaughter of the Ukrainian and Czech population took place in the village M e l y n, prov. Dubno, Volhynia. The people were driven by force into the wooden village church and b u r n e d a l i v e. Those who could find no room in the church were driven into the former town hall and burned, too. Similar incidents took place in the village of Hubkiv in the province of Kostopil, on July 2, 1943, and in many other villages of Ukraine. Besides, the Germans organized the mass shootings of the political prisoners (Rivne, Kremyanets, Kyiv, Chortkiv, Lviv, etc.) and of prominent Ukrainian intellectuals taken as hostages (Drohobych, Kovel, Kremyanets, Kryvyi Rih, Kremyanchuk etc.).

The troops of the UPA did not restrict themselves to defense. They attacked and disarmed detachments of the German army and police, captured war materials and food from German convoys, set free workers being transported to forced labor in Germany. The UPA detachments organized ambushes on principal roads and some prominent Nazis fell into their arms. In May 1943, Victor Lutze, Commander-in-Chief of the Nazi SA was killed on the highway Kovel - Brest Litovsk from an ambush along this road. In August, 1943, another detachment of UPA surrounded the concentration camp in Dubyne, near Skole in the Carpathian mountains and set free all political prisoners and killed the camp guards. Still another detachment of UPA seized the prison in Dubno, Volhynia and set free all the political prisoner inmates.

After several months of hard battles, the Germans were forced to retire to the large towns, protected by strong garrisons. The rest of the country was exclusively dominated by the UPA and administrated by Ukrainian authorities. Meanwhile agriculture and industry was developing normally, agrarian commissions appointed by the Supreme Command of UPA were dividing up large estates among poor peasants. Schools and cultural institutions operated normally. The civilian and military police of UPA kept order. The Ukrainian youth enlisted in UPA and was trained in its training camps and officer schools, operating in Volhynia and in the Carpathian mountains. Some Dutch officers, delivered from German captivity passed several weeks in one of UPA's training camps in the Carpathian mountains. With the help of the Ukrainian Resistance Movement they succeeded in escaping to Budapest from whence they returned happily to Holland. French and Serb prisoners of war, German and Italian deserters served with the Ukrainian Insurgent Army (UPA).

In the manner described above UPA became the third military and political power in Eastern Europe and soon became the champion of all revolutionary forces representing not only the resistance movement of Ukraine, but of all the subjugated peoples of

Eastern Europe, the Caucasus and Central Asia. As a result of the well planned and directed propaganda of the Supreme UPA Command the German military units composed of former German war prisoners taken on the Eastern Front began to disintegrate and filter into the ranks of UPA. A constantly increasing number of them, of Byelorussians, Georgians, Armenians, Uzbeks, Tartars Azerbaidjanians and Cossacks led to the organization of separate national legions of those peoples within the UPA. The net result of this process was the convening on November 21 and 22, 1943, in the territories then under the control of UPA, of a conference of representatives of Soviet enslaved peoples of Eastern Europe and Asia, attended by 39 delegates. The conference drew up a platform of common aims of the enslaved nationalities and adopted a common slogan: "Freedom to the peoples, freedom to the individuals"!. Thus, the Anti-Bolshevik Bloc of Nations (ABN) came into being.

The propaganda of the UPA succeeded in estranging the allies of Germans. One day all the so-called Ukrainian police of Volhynia passed with their arms to the UPA. The Hungarian, Rumanian, Slovak, French, Belgian etc. troops stationing in Ukraine were used in the expeditions against the Ukrainians. Gradually, however, the commands of these troops agreed with the Suprem Command of UPA in observing their neutrality during the Ukraino-German hostilities. Special agreement was concluded with the representatives of the Hungarian High Command in the Carpathian mountains and the friendly neutrality between Hungarian troops operating in the Carpathian mountains and the UPA was observed during the operations of Hungarian army in Eastern Galicia. This agreement was possible after heavy blows dealt to the Hungarians who initially strove to fight the Ukrainian guerillas. This agreement is now a very cordial basis of the collaboration between the Ukrainian and Hungarian resistance movements.

The Germans violently combatted UPA with their propaganda. They stated in their leaflets that the UPA was led by "Bolshevist emissaries". They tried to demonstrate to the Ukrainians that their resistance and their fight was of no use and hoped by propaganda to weaken, to corrupt and to break the fighting morale of the Ukrainian people. "Everybody who knows the gangsters, so wrote the Nazi Commissioner-General of Volhynia and Podolia to the 'working and peaceful Ukrainian population' in July, 1943, "and does not denounce them to the German authorities, will be severely punished. To save yourselves, your children, your country and your countrymen from disaster, report any gangster, or any Bandera partisan to the German authorities. The German police will protect you against their vengeance...".

But the German police could not protect their hirelings against the vengeance of the Ukrainian people and their armed forces - UPA. On Sept. 11, 1943, the chief agent of the German Gestapo and, at the same time, the agent-provocateur of NKVD Michael Tarnavskyj was captured and court-martialed by UPA. He was tried and condemned to death. There were many examples of the Nazi-Soviet collaboration in combatting UPA during that time.

The terror and propaganda of German occupational authorities in Ukraine could not break the spirit of the fighting Ukrainian people. The Ukrainian people, which has survived so many hard blows in the past, rose again against the ruthless Nazi invaders. In the beginning the Ukrainian civilian population was suffering heavy losses, because it was quite defenceless. Later the major part of the townspeople fled in the regions under the UPA's control and in these regions a system of the signalmen had secured the population against the German motorized expeditions. As in the ancient times of Tartar incursions in Ukraine, the Ukrainian population signaled by the means of bonfires the approach of the enemy. And the UPA detachments were ready and met the enemy and dealt him heavy losses. On October 8, 1943, on the road between Refalivsk and Volodymyrets detachments of the UPA encircled and annihilated a German punitive expedition, killed 300 men and captured 1 tank. On January 9, 1944, near the village Lysohirky in the province Kamyanets Podilsky in the battle against the other expedition the detachment of UPA captured 3 motor-cars, 7 machine-guns, 2 mortars, 30,000 round of ammunition and other war material. The attack against the "Black Forest" near Stanyslaviv in the Carpathian Mountains was repulsed with very high losses for the Germans.

The Germans lost in their fight against the Ukrainian Insurgent Army (UPA). During the last months of 1943 and the first months of 1944, when the Soviet counter-offensive began to roll near to Western-Ukraine, the Ukrainian Insurgent Army (UPA) consisted of four large groups: (1) UPA-North operating in Polessia and Northern Volhynia, (2) UPA-West in Eastern Galicia and in the province of Kholm, (3) UPA-South in Northern Bukovina and in the provinces of Kamyanets Podilsky and Vinnitsia, and (4) UPA-East in the wooded sector north of Kyiv and Zhitomir, in the area of Bazar - the battle-field of famous Ukrainian anti-Bolshevik uprising in 1921. These 4 groups comprised more than 200,000 armed Ukrainian guerillas which were united under one command - the Supreme Command of the UPA. Besides, the Ukrainian Resistance Movement organized the underground combat groups in the Donets Basin, Dnipropetrovsk, Dniprodzerzhynsk, Kryvyi Rih, Odessa, Kremenchuk, Kyiv, Uman and other towns of Ukraine and the peninsula of Crimea. The chief of the Ukrainian Resistance Movement at those times was MAXYM RUBAN as the substitute of STEPAN BANDERA who was then in the concentration camp of Sachsenhausen. The Supreme Commander of the Ukrainian Insurgent Army (UPA) was Col. Roman Klashkivsky (Klym Savur), his chief of staff was Gen. Anathol Stupnytzky (Moncharenko). Both officers fell in the fight against the Bolsheviks.   General Stupnytzky, former colonel of the Ukrainian Army, 1918-1921 and the hero of an anti-Bolshevist uprising in 1921 was chiefly responsible for the development of the military strength of the UPA. He and his collaborators indefatigably worked on the organization of the UPA, on its training and supplies and on leading its operations.

The growth of the UPA went hand-in-hand with the growth of the OUN, the sole important political organization in Ukraine during the German occupation and at present. But the second occupation of Ukraine by the Soviets raised the apprehension that this occupation would turn out to be of long duration. The general strategy of the Ukrainian Resistance Movement had, therefore, to be broadened and laid out accordingly. First of all, however, full national unity had to be secured. It became evident that the Supreme Command of the Ukrainian struggle for liberation could not rest in the hands of only one party. This conclusion was reached as a result of the development in Ukraine during the times of German occupation there. In very short time the UPA lost the appearance of a guerilla organization of one political party and became all-national in its character. The ranks of the UPA were swollen with Ukrainian peasants, workers and intellectuals who were not members of the OUN. Thus, the UPA became an armed organization of the whole

Ukrainian people, common to all, in which the whole people participated and took pride. Even the most indifferent obeyed the orders of the UPA, regarding it as the true Ukrainian rule. Thus, the general consolidation of the Ukrainian people into one military camp was brought about.

Granted this situation, the necessity arose to give an outward expression of this internal consolidation by the formation of a supreme directing body. It was necessary that a supreme political and state organ should crown the national struggle, in which all forces and elements taking part would be represented. In July, 1944, a Ukrainian National Congress was summoned in the territory occupied by the UPA. This Congress gave birth to the SUPREME LIBERATION COUNCIL (ukr. UHVR), as the supreme state organ of the Ukrainian nation for the duration of its struggle for freedom and sovereignty. This Council was built on democratic principles. Its executive is the General Secretariate. At the head of each department there is a General Secretary. The aim and purposes of the Council are expressed in its Constitution and its Proclamation to the Ukrainian people. Some extracts of this Proclamation are quoted below.

Ukrainian People!

... It is not in the cause of your freedom that the imperialistic aggrandizers are waging this bloody and cruel war. For you they bring only ruin, enslavement and death. You did not allow yourselves to become enslaved but demonstrated an unyielding determination to live in independent statehood on your native land. On guard over your freedom, you have set up - from the Carpathian peaks beyond the Don to the Caucasus - armed cadres of your sons - the Ukrainian Insurgent Army.

... In order to unite all national-liberation elements of the Ukrainian people, in order to direct their struggle for freedom from one common center, in order to represent their political will before the world... the Supreme Ukrainian Liberation Council has been brought into being...

... The Supreme Ukrainian Liberation Council is the supreme and sole governing organ of the Ukrainian people during the time of their revolutionary struggle and up to the time of the establishment of a government of a Ukrainian Independent and Sovereign State...

... The Supreme Ukrainian Liberation Council swears before you, Ukrainian People, that:

> It will fight to make you the sole master of your soul,
> For a just social order without oppression and exploitation,
> For the destruction of serfdom,
> For free enterprise of the peasant on his own land,
> For free enterprise for the worker,
> For wide initiative of the working people in all branches of the economic order,
> For the widest possible development of the Ukrainian national culture.

... The Supreme Ukrainian Liberation Council greets the struggle of enslaved peoples for their liberation. The Ukrainian people desire to live with them, particularly with their neighbors, in neighborly friendship and to collaborate with them in the struggle against common enemies...

... Our liberation struggle demands heroism and bloody sacrifices, and above all unshakable faith in our own truth...

... The heroic struggle of your ancestors and the memory of their knightly death in the cause of Ukrainian statehood - is a dictate to you.

We therefore call upon you: Rise and fight for your freedom and for your nation. Unite yourselves in your struggle, and strengthen your spirit.

SUPREME UKRAINIAN LIBERATION COUNCIL

Headquarters, June, 1944.

(Note: The Supreme Ukrainian Liberation Council met in the Carpathian mountains on July 7-14, 1944, on the territory under control of the Ukrainian Insurgent Army. From 36 elected members, 20 Ukrainian political leaders appeared and participated in this meeting. They represented all Ukrainian lands, religions, and parties which stood on the principle of the underground revolutionary fight against both invaders of Ukraine. For the reasons of conspiracy all documents of the First Meeting of the Supreme Ukrainian Liberation Council are dated with June, 1944).

In addition to the quoted declaration and its constitution the Council worked out a political p r o g r a m for the entire Ukrainian Resistance Movement. The program envisages a democratic process of installing government in a free Ukraine, and reserves for the Ukrainian people the right to choose their own form of government, the form of social-economical order and the form of local government in a Constituent Assembly which is to be convoked after the overthrowing of Russian Bolshevism and its rule in Ukraine. "The present communist system", states the program, "alien to Ukrainian tradition and repugnant to the spirit of the people is to be replaced by a system of cooperatives, which have proved themselves very popular in Ukraine".

The Supreme Ukrainian Liberation Council chose the members of the General Secretariat and delegated to the President of the General Secretariat, Gen. Taras CHUPRYNKA, the responsibility for all operations of the Ukrainian Insurgent Army (UPA). He was appointed Supreme Commander of the UPA and is holding this post up to now. In addition the Supreme Ukrainian Liberation Council made provision for its administrative organs and the method of their election. According to its constitution the center of the Supreme Ukrainian Liberation Council (SUCL- ukr.UHVR) always must be in Ukraine and only its delegations are sent abroad. At the present time the Foreign Representation of the Supreme Ukrainian Liberation Council consists of 12 members.

Soviet propaganda pretended that the Ukrainian revolutionaries (UHVR - UPA - OUN) were tools of the Nazis. They have never explained why these Nazi tools fought long after the Germans had gone and long before the Germans came. The lie that the Ukrainians were working with the Nazis is disproved by the reports in the captured German archives, showing the trouble they had with the Ukrainian Resistance Movement and its Ukrainian Insurgent Army (UPA). It is proved by the order of the day issued by Gen. Taras Chuprynka - Commander-in-Chief of the Ukrainian Insurgent Army (UPA) on VE Day. The original text of General Chuprynka's Order appeared in an UPA underground magazine, "Povstanets" (The Insurgent), No. 5-6 for April-May, 1945. In speaking to his men, he spoke for practically the entire Ukrainian nation and for the world:

Fighting Men and Commanders of the Ukrainian Insurgent Army!

Hitler's Germany has found its final and irrevocable destruction.

The Ukrainian people will no longer fear death in gas chambers or liquidation of their entire villages by the Gestapo. No more will the German hit the freedom-loving Ukrainian peasants in the face, nor take his land in order to turn him into a slave for the German master. No longer will the Germans be able to drive thousands and tens of thousands of peasants and workers into modern slavery in Germany. Nor will the Ukrainian intellectual worker have to wait his turn to be liquidated because he always and ever has been a menace to the invader. The barbarian from the West no longer will dominate over the Ukrainian land.

A great contribution toward the victory over Germany was made by you, Ukrainian Insurgents. You prevented the German from freely exploiting the Ukrainian soil and using its fruits for his aggressive designs. You prohibited his pillaging of Ukrainian villages, you fought the forced deportations to Germany. Your retributive hand repaid the German for mass executions and burning of villages. In the struggle against Germany our Ukrainian Insurgent Army was first organized and received its fighting training.

But with the defeat and collapse of Germany an even worse invader has come back to Ukraine - Russia. For centuries enslaving Ukraine, Russia whether ruled by the Tsars or by the "most democratic regime in the world", - that Russia has always had sinister and impérialistic designs upon our country. This so-called "socialistic republic", has finally decided to put an end to the aspirations of the Ukrainian people for liberty and independence. Having enchained all its people in a new social system of state capitalism, the ruling clique has created such unbearable economic conditions that under it the freedom-loving man has become a perpetually hungry beast with no problem on his mind but food. Having introduced a new culture, "national in form, but socialist in content", the Soviet government, with the help of such terrorized Ukrainian slaves as Tychyna, Bazhan, Vyshnia and Voznisk - forcibly injects Russian culture into Ukraine. To mislead still further the Ukrainian people, the Soviet government has even created the Commissariat of Defence and that of Foreign Affairs, which have no other tasks or duties but to glorify Stalin. By the most inhuman terror mankind has ever known and by insidious provocations, it attempts to boil the Ukrainian people in a Russian pot, so that the Ukrainians should forget that they once were free and indepéndent, and that without protest they should accept being eternal slaves of the "elder brother" - of the new and powerful Russia. For those who reject this Russian culture, "the most democratic republic" has the Siberian Taygas, the Solovatski Islands, mass executions, the burning of villages, state-instigated famine and other "modern methods of education".

But the Ukrainian people have not and will not ever capitulate before the enemy. In 1943 they gave you, Ukrainian Insurgents, weapons into your hands with the explicit order to defend to the last the ideal of Ukrainian freedom and independence. With superb determination and heroism, with unheard of faith and devotion, you have been fighting for this ideal for more than two years. Neither hunger nor privation, nor terror applied to your families has shaken your intrepidity and your belief in the final victory. At all the deceitful approaches and addresses of the "Government of the Ukrainian Soviet Socialist Republic", you have strengthened your effort. You remember only too well that by such methods Russia tried to demoralize and weaken the brave soldiers of Mazepa; the same insidious propaganda was used in the years 1920-1943 by the Soviets in order to entice those from among us who were naive enough to believe them. All those who trusted the Russians were "rewarded" by being sent to slave labor camps or executed as soon as their usefulness to Russia came to an end. When you embarked upon the struggle with the Stalinist regime, you knew that we could not capitualte because the enemy that menaces the very existence of the nation, must be fought until victory or death comes. I am certain that the weapons given you by your people will not be covered with dishonor, and you will leave your names covered with immortal glory for posterity.

Ukrainian Insurgents!

The world has no peace as yet. The revolutionary movements of the oppressed peoples as well as the antagonism between the western democracies and the USSR will increase. The people the world over will become increasingly aware what the "dictatorship of the proletariat", formulated in and propagated by the Kremlin, means to humanity. In the struggle against the Kremlin you are by no means alone. The brave Serbs and Croats continue to fight Tito who is nothing but a tool of Moscow; the Bulgarians also are rebelling against the bloody terror brought to the country by the "allied" USSR. The mountains of Transylvania are overcrowded with those Russians who have refused to submit to Russia. Even little Slovakia has a regular guerilla warfare against the invader. The Polish patriots by constant sabotage and armed struggle fight all the attempts of Stalin to enslave them. The ranks of fighters against the Oriental satrap are increasing daily. All this, of course, creates favorable conditions for continuing our struggle and brings nearer the moment of downfall for the USSR.

To be able to survive to that moment with the weapons in your hands and to give leadership to all those fighting Stalin - this is your sacred duty. I have a firm belief that you will fulfil it with honor and determination as you have fulfilled all your previous tasks and duties. By using the new methods of struggle, adaptable to the new conditions, you will give a resolute answer to the challenging enemy.

Onward with unshakeable faith!

Long live the Independent and Sovereign Ukrainian state!

Glory be to those who fall fighting the invader!

Glory to Ukraine!

Taras CHUPRYNKA, General
Commander-in-Chief of the
Ukrainian Insurgent Army

Headquarters, May 1945

Such was the Ukrainian Resistance Movement at the time of the German occupation of Ukraine and such was the Ukrainian underground government which came into being on the eve of Soviet reoccupation of Ukraine. For the great part of the Ukrainian people it is now a true Ukrainian government opposing to "quisling" Soviet-Ukrainian government of Khrushchev, Manuilsky, etc. As such it is recognized by the Ukrainian Insurgent Army (UPA) and by the broad masses of the Ukrainian population. The best proof that this statement is no exaggeration is the fact that the Ukrainian people united in the revolutionary Army (UPA) and under the leadership of the Supreme Ukrainian Liberation Council has been proudly offering stern opposition to the powerful Soviet-Union for four years now since the end of military operations in Europe. The Ukrainian Resistance Movement is spreading all over Ukraine and beyond the borders of Ukraine, appearing from time to time in Poland, Czechoslovakia, Yugoslavia and Byelorussia. Its aim is to coordinate the underground action of the other peoples enslaved by the Soviets and it is succeeding in it, because in their fight of long duration the Ukrainian Resistance Movement was sole to develop the best methods and to create the most convincing ideology of the struggle against the Bolshevist totalitarianism. This fact places the Ukrainian Resistance Movement in a **prominent position** among the enslaved nations of Eastern Europe and Central Asia as well as the "Satellite" nations under the sphere of influence.

The rulers of the Kremlin are fully aware of the danger on the part of the Ukrainian Resistance Movement. At the 16th Ukrainian Communist Party Congress in Kyiv (January 1949) Mr. David Manuilsky, Foreign Minister of the Ukrainian SSR called the delegates for constant vigilance against "nationalist distortions" on Ukrainian home front. He spoke in the course of a general discussion following the main report delivered the previous day by Ukrainian communist Party Secretary General Nikita Khrushchev. Mr. Khrushchev had called the delegates to intensify the struggle against the "Ukrainian bourgeois nationalism" which has not ceased to exist after 31 years of Soviet rule in Ukraine. Having in mind that usually the Soviet leaders are very scarce on such statements, the free world must realize that this "Ukrainian nationalism" is a very concrete factor in Eastern European affairs and that it became once more "a grave danger" for the mighty Soviet-Union.

6. The Ukrainian Resistance Movement versus the Kremlin (1944-1949)

By Spring, 1944, after the collapse of the German front in Ukraine, the German commanders in Ukraine hastened to make contact with the troops of the UPA and proposed an anti-Bolshevist collaboration with them. But any negotiations with the Germans were interdicted by the Supreme UPA command. By autumn, 1944, when nearly all of the territory of Ukraine was occupied by the Soviet army, the German policy entirely changed; the German press was full of praises of the UPA for their anti-Bolshevist successes and the UPA fighters were now called "Ukrainian fighters for freedom", although some months before the same press had called them "Ukrainian national brigands". The leader of the German sponsored Russian "Vlassov Army" in his interview given to the international pressmen, which was printed in "Völkischer Beobachter" on Dec. 7, 1944, confirmed the importance and the strength of the UPA and stressed the efforts of this army in its fight against the Bolshevists. But it was already too late.

When the Soviet armies began launching their offensives against the Germans, and the latter began rolling back from Ukraine, the UPA utilized the German retreat to gather as many weapons as possible for its own use. The troops of the UPA attacked and disarmed the retiring detachments of the German and Hungarian army and police, capturing weapons fighting vehicles, clothing, footwear, and other war material and seizing ordnance stores of arms and ammunition. When the Soviet war machine began to roll over the territory occupied by the UPA, the latter could meet the new enemy fully prepared for the struggle and well-armed.

It must be emphasized that, at this time, the UPA detachments did not fight against the Red Army which, in this area consisted chiefly of Ukrainians (i.e. the armies of the 1st, 2nd, 3rd, and 4th Ukrainian front). They only defended themselves, preferring to circulate among the Red soldiers and to distribute leaflets which were prepared by the hundreds of thousands and which summoned the soldiers of the Red Army to fight against Hitler and Stalin. The activity of the UPA also was directed against the restoration of Soviet military and civilian authorities. The UPA systematically opposed the mobilization of Ukrainians into the Red Army. It routed the NKVD units by sudden raids on administration centers which caused heavy personnel losses for the new occupants. This action was leveled against the local Red spies and collaborators, as well as agents of the NKVD among the local population. Simultaneously, the UPA opposed the restoration of the collective farms and the sending out of Ukrainian wheat and other foodstuffs, as well as the deportation of the Ukrainian population into semi-slave labor camps in Donbas (Donets Basin) or farther North and East.

At the time, when the Soviet war machine was engaged in the fight against the Nazis, the Soviets could not organize a serious military action against the UPA. Several times the Soviet government presented an ultimatum to the UPA ordering the Ukrainian insurgents to surrender and promising amnesty. Soon the Soviets realized that the only thing which could crush the UPA would be for the Soviet government to exile the whole of the Western Ukrainian population to Siberia and to replace them with Russians. By spring and Summer, 1945, the Soviets began their famous deportations of the Ukrainian population to Siberia and Kazakhstan. The UPA was forced to resort to arms. At this time, its activities reached the proportions of a war. To counter the activity of the UPA, the Soviets organized and launched their first great offensive against the UPA which was personally led by Premier Khrushchev and "Ukrainian" Minister of the NKVD, Gen.Lt.Ryassny. This offensive, called Khrushchev - Ryassny offensive, lasted from Spring to Autumn of 1945. It was a series of attacks and puses and was a hard kind of fighting to the UPA. The Soviets used aeroplanes, artillery, tanks, blocked villages, roads, and forests. They tried to encircle the groups of the Ukrainian insurgents and to annihilate them. The latter defended themselves by mining roads, railway tracks, natural cross roads and even stream-beds. Several battles were given by the Ukrainian insurgents in the forests of the Subcarpathian region and in the Carpathian mountains.

The great offensive led by Khrushchev-Ryassny could not break the resistance of the UPA. The battailons and companies of the UPA withdrew to the Carpathian mountains and from there continued their fight against the Communist oppressors. Small groups of fighters remained in the country. Having hid in the underground bunkers and shelters, they made sudden raids on the administrative centers and NKVD posts or by ambushing military transportation facilities, columns, or convoys. Railway trains were destroyed by exploding the roadbed or removing trackage. Before an attack all telephone communications were usually destroyed.

By October 1945, this offensive against UPA ended. The Bolsheviks were taken aback by the strength of the UPA and by the support given it by the Ukrainian population. They were surprised by the slight success of the general amnesty they proclaimed in the country, and at the insignificant success of their big action against the UPA. But mostly they were surprised at the behaviour of the units of the Red Army which were used in this action. And this behaviour was the chief reason for suddenly halting this action in autumn, 1945.

When the Soviets planned their action against the UPA, they decided to attract to this action the units of the Red Army which were on the move from West to East after Germany's defeat. In connection with that, the Soviets developed a special plan of march through the Western Ukraine. The most confidential troops have lodged for a long time throughout the country with the task of helping the "interior" police troops (NKVD-MKGB) break the resistance of the Ukrainian population. In executing this plan, however, the Soviets have not succeeded at all. The UPA opposed not only with passionate armed defence, but also developed an uncommonly strong political campaign which began to influence the Red Army's troops garrisoned in Ukraine. The freedom-loving, revolutionary, progressive slogans of the UPA program, which disclosed all the falseness and evil of the Bolshevist Totalitarian Dictatorship, found a broad lively echo among the Red Army's soldiers, who had just returned from the front. They, themselves, saw in Europe quite another reality from the Soviet one, and now attentively listened to the voice of the UPA. The Red Army's soldiers, and very often the whole Red Army's detachment were not willing to take part in huntings and terroristic actions directed against the UPA and the Ukrainian population. And whenever they were obliged to take part in such actions, they, very often, did it only outwardly, endeavoring not to meet the UPA formations, not to fight them and even very often aided the UPA with information and weapons.

The Soviets dismayed by these facts, were obliged to withdraw the Red Army troops from any direct actions against the UPA and have never used them since that time. They had to withdraw the demoralized troops of the Red Army from Ukraine and to replace them with more disciplined and trustworthy troops. From all parts of the Soviet-Union they brought the fresh divisions of the MVD-MGB security police into the Western Ukraine. The best units of the MVD-MGB troops were selected in the Far East region, Siberia, the Leningrad area, and having passed a special training, were thrown into the fight against the UPA. At least 15 divisions of the MVD-MGB troops were concentrated in the Sub-carpathian area and in Volhynia with the purpose of annihilation of the UPA. These units were composed of young Bolsheviks, fanatics who were told that they were going to fight the "remnants" of German "fascists", SS-men, members of the most hated "Vlassov Army" and other original elements which were hiding in the Carpathian mountains. They were asked to fight the "people's enemies" without any respect to sex, age, etc. Most barbarous methods were permitted; pillaging the country, murdering the population, and ravishing the girls. There were special units from Siberia which consisted of men ill with Siberian syphilis. They were designed to spread this kind of syphilis among the Ukrainian population and for this purpose they were allowed to rape even the young girls to infect them with this frightful disease.

The "Ukrainian" Minister of the Interior Gen.Lt. Ryassny took responsibility for carrying out a new action and Gen.Col.Moskalenko was appointed chief commander of the MVD-MGB troops designed for it. The second big action against the UPA began in the middle of December, 1945, and lasted till the end of June, 1946. It was called Ryassny-Moskalenko offensive.

Meanwhile, the Ukrainian Resistance Movement made preparations for the "electoral" campaign for the Supreme Soviet of the USSR which was to be held on Febr. 10, 1946. In order to show the Ukrainian people that the Ukrainian Resistance Movement had not been liquidated by the action of Khrushchev-Ryassny in 1945, the battalions of the UPA made a sudden raid on the provincial center of Stanislav (120,000 inhabitants) in the Subcarpathian area on Oct. 31, 1945, and seized it doing much harm to the Soviet occupiers. This attack was conducted by 5 UPA batalions at night and caused a big panic among the Bolsheviks and brought great satisfaction to the Ukrainian population.

Knowing the character of Soviet "elections", the Supreme Ukrainian Liberation Council decided to boycott the elections to the Supreme Soviet of the USSR and summoned the Ukrainian people not to take part in these elections. The Ukrainian Resistance Movement started an "anti-electoral" campaign with the result that the Ukrainians of the Western Ukraine did not go to vote.

The Soviet "electoral" campaign has nothing in common with the democratic electoral campaign. As there is, in the USSR, only one official party, the Soviet "electoral" campaign is only a planned manoeuvre of the official Communist Party to strengthen and fortify its psychological pressure on the masses of the population and to terrorize them both psychologically and physically. The official electoral propaganda campaign has the task of terrifying, hypnotizing and mobilizing the masses of the population and, in this way, make them flexible, dumb, and obedient instruments in the hands of the official party clique.

As it is not allowed to put forward a non-official candidate, no anti-electoral propaganda is not allowed. Such propaganda was possible only in the form of an active, persistent and organized mass struggle, including the armed resistance of the UPA. It had to defend the citizens against the terrorism and state police and special troops which had the task of forcing them to participate in the elections. Thus, the boycott of the Soviet elections, proclaimed by the Supreme Ukrainian Liberation Council soon was transformed into a wide and very persistent fight of the Ukrainian people against the Soviet occupiers.

This fight began already in the middle of December, 1945, and took on very large proportions. The MVD-MGB troops of Ryassny - Moskalenko were already concentrated in the Western Ukraine, and on a given signal they began the fight on December 18, 1945.

For a month before the beginning of this action an "order" of Gen.Lt. Ryassny was distributed in the country. It is reproduced here in full. Of course there were not many people in Ukraine so naive that they were deluded by this merry song of the NKVD siren.

ORDER
of People's Commissar of Internal Affairs of the Ukrainian SSR
15th November, 1945   City of Kyiv

A great number of partisans have recently come voluntarily to the organs of NKVD, and have said that they could not arrive before the 20th of July, this year, which has been fixed as the last term by the government of the Ukrainian SSR.

One of the chief reasons that the people could not arrive in on time, they state, was the fact that, although they wanted to break with the partisans and apply to the organs of the Soviet administration, they were not able to do that, because the conditions of their actual abode were such that they were not allowed to go out.

In addition to the partisans, a great number of Red Army deserters are arriving to join the organs of NKVD.

Upon these statements

I Order

all members of partisan bands who have left their partisan activities and who could not arrive only because of the above mentioned conditions as well as those, who have avoided mobilization into the Red Army

will not be subject to any reprisals and will be directed immediately to their places of residence.

People's Commissar of Internal Affairs
of Ukrainian SSR
(Signed) Gen.Lt. V. Ryassny

After the 18th of December, 1945, military detachments of the interior police, troops of MVD-MGB, and special selected troops of the Red Army continued garrisoning in every locality of the Western Ukraine and even in every village and in the smallest hamlets of several huts. The number of garrisoned military troops ranged from 10 men in the smallest hamlets to 300-500 men in bigger localities. The only job of those police-military troops was to spread violence and terror. In the woods and forests incessant searches for the Ukrainian insurgents took place. The prisons were being filled up with more and more prisoners often arrested for only suspicion of an anti-official attitude. And under such conditions, the Ukrainian anti-electoral campaign was carried on successfully by means of: (a) conspirational talks and small conspirational meetings, (b) clandestine spreading of proclamations, short written instructions and calls, (c) whispered propaganda, (d) posting in visible places of manifestos and appeals of the Supreme Ukrainian Liberation Council and of the UPA, (e) open mass meetings, speeches and open distributing of manifestos and appeals under the protection of the detachments of the UPA, (f) breaking up of official meetings and changing them into anti-official ones.

During the time of the "electoral campaign" one and a half thousand battles and combats against Red troops were fought by the UPA. 5000 officers and soldiers of the UPA were killed and wounded in action. The Bolsheviks lost, at least, 15,000 men killed and wounded, but the Ukrainian people did not go to vote!

In a majority of the villages, especially in the western provinces of Ukraine nobody went to the elections at all. Because of that many terroristic acts of violence occurred. The soldiers of garrisoned military-police troops maltreated the people to compel them to go into electoral halls and throw into urns the electoral bulletins. They shot at the fleeing people and killed many Ukrainians. They set on fire the houses of the opponents. Finally, they, themselves, threw as many electoral bulletins as they wanted into the urns. We are in possession of hundreds of murders perpetrated against the Ukrainian people who were not willing to take part in the "elections".

The Ukrainian people used the day of "elections" as a unanimous demonstration against the Soviet totalitarian dictatorship. They showed that they were not willing to take part in these elections because they were striving for liberty and freedom in their own independent state. The Ukrainians boycotted the elections under a slogan of protestation against the suppression of Ukraine and other subjugated peoples, and against the reign of terror and violence. In an anti-election appeal we read: "Communists lie all over the world that the Ukrainian Soviet Socialist Republic is a free and independent nation. We shall retort to this common lie with a general boycott of elections. We are obliged to tell the world that we are against the dictatorship and tyranny. Long live true democracy! Long live free elections in a Ukrainian United Independent State!"

The Soviets falsified the election returns, stating that 99% of the voters participated in the elections. In the rayon Woynyliv, prov. Stanislav, 10,672 persons were eligible to vote. Of this number only 176 voted voluntarily, 599 were forced to vote, and 9,897 did not vote at all. Nevertheless, the Soviets trumpeted a great "election victory" in this rayon and reported a 99,8% vote in this area.

On of the principal actions of the Ukrainian Resistance Movement which took place after the "elections", was the opposition to the forced re-union of the Ukrainian Catholic Church with Russian Orthodox Church as announced by Moscow on March 17, 1946. Ukrainian Catholics in Western Ukraine were being deported, imprisoned, subjected to forced labor, or killed, if they refused to join the Orthodox Church. In connection with this persecution a proclamation of the Supreme Ukrainian Liberation Council stated: "Neither the Red divisions which were against the UPA nor the bloody terror of the Russian-Gestapo-NKVD could break the Ukrainian resistance. We are convinced that Russian orthodoxy under the leadership of Russian police NKVD will not subjugate the spirit of the Ukrainian resistance. Suppression of religion, and the introduction of Orthodoxy by means of force, will only strengthen the front of our struggle and will widen its perspective..." Of course, the Supreme Ukrainian Liberation Council issued orders forbidding the forced apostasy and asking the priests and faithful to oppose the Bolshevik pogrom against the Ukrainian Catholic Church.

This pogrom began as early as 1945 when the Catholic Church was denounced in the press in Kyiv and Lviv, and other Ukrainian cities. The Pope's Christmas message on "True and False Democracy" was bitterly attacked, and the Pope was labeled an "abetter of fascism". In April, 1945, an article entitled "With Cross and Knife" by Volodymyr Rosovych appeared in the Soviet-Ukrainian papers in Lviv and Kyiv. The article attacked the late Metropolitan Sheptytsky as the "servant of reactionary Rome". He asserted that the Ukrainian Catholic Church and its clergy, in league with the Vatican, were supporting the Ukrainian Resistance Movement against the Soviet system, and therefore could not be tolerated.

x of many protocols about thousands of cases of maltreatment, many

Following these verbal sallies actual physical attacks began. We reproduce here eye-witness reports printed in the publication "For An Independent State", (No.9-10), which appears clandestinely somewhere in Ukraine: "On April 11, 1945, a special detachment of NKVD troops surrounded the St.George Cathedral in Lviv. After a thorough search, according to the best methods of NKVD, the following were arrested: Metropolitan Joseph Slipy, Bishop Nicitas Budka, Bishop Nicholas Charnetzky; the prelates, Rev. O. Kovalsky and Rev. L. Kunitsky; Reverends Gorchynyky, Beley, Sampara, Rector of the Theological Seminary, Rev. Bilyk, Director of a Catholic School, and Rev. Hodunka, who after brutal tortures, died few days after his arrest. The students of the Theological Seminary were rounded up and put in a camp on Pieracki street. All the professors of the Theological Seminary were herded into a meeting organized by the NKVD, and informed that the Ukrainian Catholic Church had ceased to exist, that its Metropolitan had been arrested, and St.George Cathedral would be taken over by the Orthodox bishop appointed by the Soviet authorities. During the search the NKVD men conducted themselves in a brutal manner and took all gold and silver objects, liturgical wine, etc."

These raids were carried on throughout the Western Ukraine. All Ukrainian Catholic bishops were arrested. In Stanislav, the NKVD arrested Bishop Gregory Khomyshyn and his auxiliary Bishop Latishevsky. In Peremyshl, which nominally does not belong to the Ukrainian SSR but rather to Poland of Bierut & Co, the NKVD arrested Bishop Josaphat Kocylovsky, together with his auxiliary, Bishop Gregory Lakota. Of these Ukrainian Catholic prelates at least two, namely, Bishop Khomyshyn and Kotsylovsky were reported dead in Soviet dungeons, while others are working under the strict supervision of the MVD in the Vorkuta coal mines in the Soviet subarctic region. In the fall of 1947 the last Catholic Bishop of Ukraine, Bishop Theodore Romzha of Carpatho-Ukraine met his tragic death in an "accident" with a Soviet army tank.

After the pogrom against the Ukrainian Catholic hierarchy, the Russians went on to liquidate the lesser clergy. But out of a total of 3600 Ukrainian Catholic priests only 42 had submitted to the apostasy by the end of June, 1945. Finally on March 8th, 1946, a "synod" convened at Lviv. It was headed by those Ukrainian priests who have submitted to the apostasy and "officially" proclaimed the "reunion" of the Ukrainian Catholic Church with the Russian Orthodox Church. But the Supreme Ukrainian Liberation Council stated that this "synod" was illegal and its decisions invalid, because, according to canon law, only bishops had the right to convene such ecclesiastic meetings. There are reports that among 216 "priests" attending this "synod" the majority were Russian NKVD agents disguised as Catholic priests.

In connection with this pogrom of the Ukrainian Catholic Church, the Supreme Ukrainian Liberation Council submitted to the Holy See a memorandum in regard to the persecution of the Ukrainian Catholic Church in Ukraine asking the Holy See: (1) To designate an exarch for the Ukrainian Catholic Church in Western parts of Ukraine until all Bishops and priests should be released from Soviet prisons, (2) To make every effort for the liberation of Ukrainian Bishops and priests from Soviet prisons, (3) To take a canonical stand in regard to the so-called "reunion" of the Ukrainian Catholic Church with the Russian Orthodox Church, (4) To ask the United Nations to send a mixed commission to investigate the "voluntary" transference of the Ukrainian Catholic Church to the Russian Orthodox Church and (5) To nominate a Field Bishop for the Ukrainian Insurgent Army (UPA).

Here we must point out that the mock trial of Cardinal Mindszenty in which the venerable prelate was condemned to life imprisonment on trumped-up charges by Stalin's communist puppets now in power in Budapest was an exact replica of the so-called "purge" trials long in operation in Soviet Russia. Only after tortures and druggings, which are commonplace practices under Soviet Russia's judicial system, was Cardinal Mindszenty allowed to appear before the court as a morally and physically broken men. The trials against the Ukrainian Catholic bishops were announced by the Soviets, but the bishops themselves did not appear before the court because no tortures and druggings could break their spirit, and they did not confess to the crimes they had not committed. We can only be surprised at the fact, that the whole world remained calm and silent when the Bolsheviks imprisoned all the Ukrainian Catholic Bishops because they had refused to apostate their faith, and when the Ukrainian clergy and the faithful were persecuted and arrested because they had refused to be separated from their true mother church. The New York Times of August 5, 1949, printed a letter by Most Rev. Ivan Buchko, D.D. Apostolic Visitator for the Ukrainians in Western Europe, about the large-scale persecution of clergy and laity in Ukraine by the Soviet authorities. The letter, sent from Rome and dated July 20, 1949, read:

"For some time I have been reading editorials of The New York Times and other American newspapers that reach me about the persecution of the Catholic Church and her hierarchy by the Soviets and their satellites. I am surprised and deeply regret that nothing has been mentioned of the liquidation of the Ukrainian Catholic Church in Western Ukraine and Carpatho-Ukraine, which has been persecuted for so long.

"The tragic fate of Cardinal Mindszenty and of Archbishop Stepinac is well known, as well as the recent persecution of Archbishop Joseph Beran of Prague. But hardly anything is known of the fact that the entire Ukrainian Catholic hierarchy has been completely liquidated. Some bishops are dead, others are still suffering in the Soviet camps, where they are assigned to hard labor.

"The cruel hand of the Soviets fell upon them during the night of April 11, 1945. All of them had long been singled out as church leaders and patriots, firmly believing in the cause of Ukrainian national independence. All were arrested on the same night and within a short time - hundreds of priests and faithful as well. Convenient tools were soon found, who "dissolved" the Ukrainian Catholic Church as such and made it a part of the Russian Orthodox Church under the leadership of the Kremlin-dominated Patriarch of Moscow.

"His Holiness, Pope Pius, in his famous encyclical, Orientales Omnes, called the attention of the world to the martyrdom of the Ukrainian Catholic Church under the Soviet regime and appealed to all Christians to pray for the Ukrainian Catholics.

"The Ukrainian Catholic Church was the first, but not the last, to fall a victim of the Muscovite war against Rome. Nonetheless, according to reports that still reach us here, the religious spirit of the Ukrainians and their national fervor burn brighter than ever before."

Under the protection of the Ukrainian Resistance Movement the free Ukrainian Catholic Church continues to exist in the Western Ukraine. The Ukrainian Catholic Church went underground and in this way fulfills the religious needs of the Ukrainian population. Moreover, it has widened the scope of its activities and spread all over Ukraine.

Meanwhile the big Ryassny-Moskalenko offensive was rolling over the Subcarpathian area with the purpose of totally annihilating the UPA. But even then, it was a hard task to fight it. By Spring 1946, all the forests of the Western Ukraine, such as the Tsumansky forest near Kovel, the Yaniv forest near Lviv, and the Black forest near Stanislav, were burnt down in order to deprive the Ukrainian insurgents of their natural bases. In this case the devastation was immense. In order to infect the populations the Soviets sold serums of typhus and other bacteria on the black market where the medicines for the UPA were bought, despite the fact that bacteorological warfare was outlawed by international treaties, and even the Hitlerites did not use such methods in combatting the UPA.

On May 3, 1946, Gen.Col.Moskalenko, one colonel, and two majors were shot in an armored car near the railway station of Tisziv, prov.Stanislav, by an UPA subdetachment of "Avengers". Secret collaborators had informed the UPA detachment of the exact time of the departure of the commander-in-chief of the anti-UPA movement and his staff officers from Stanislav for Stryj. The armored car was hit from ambush at close range by missiles from an insurgent "bazooka". The UPA sub-detachment was attacked by the convoy of the NKVD general and was forced to withdraw to the nearest forest. This incident was reported only by the illegal magazine of the Supreme Ukrainian Liberation Council, "Samostiynist" (Independence), in the summer 1946 issue p.159.

About the end of June, 1946, the garrisons of the MVD-MGB troops withdrew from the country. As usual the Soviets announced their "great victory" over the "remnants" of "Ukrainian-German" nationalists and proclaimed the "definite liquidation" of the "Ukrainian partisan bands". But the Soviet leader, responsible for this action, Gen.Lt.Ryassny, got neither the Kutuzov nor the Suvorov medal for this "victory". He was relieved of his post as Minister of the Interior of the Ukrainian SSR and replaced by Gen. Kruhlov, former Minister of the Interior of the USSR. This was the best proof that the Ryassny "victory" was no victory at all. The MVD-MGB detachments "succeeded" in killing many Ukrainian civilians, and in devastating the country, but it was a very hypothetical "victory". It caused only an unlimited hatred of the Ukrainian people for the Soviet-muscovite methods of combatting the UPA. And these methods were worthy of their masters. All the horrors of the times of Ivan the Terrible or Peter the Great were revived in the Western Ukraine.

The Ukrainian Resistance Movement has survived the terrible offensive of the Ryassny-Moskalenko forces and has shown to Ukraine and to the world that there are limits of terror. It has shown that determined people are able to withstand the pressure of overwhelming enemy forces who know no pardon. It has shown the world that such people are even able to win their fight as they know what they are fighting for.

The significance of the survival of the Ukrainian Resistance Movement is immense. By its survival the Ukrainian Resistance Movement has shown that an underground revolutionary-political fight against the Soviet colossus is possible. Its armed groups

not only protected the Ukrainian population before the terror of
the Soviet secret police, but it also paralyzed all efforts of
the oppressors to carry out their occupation policies. By the
solidarity, sacrifices and fanatic heroism of its fighters, the
Ukrainian Resistance Movement gained the admiration of the whole
Ukrainian people and even of its opponents, and succeeded in
calling the whole Ukrainian people to the struggle against the
bloody usurpers.

Nevertheless, the Ukrainian Resistance Movement became aware
that it had to change from a mass underground to an individual
conspiracy. It had to replace the breadth of the movement with
depth, the extensiveness with intensity, the quantity with
quality. The Ukrainian Resistance Movement had to become a body
with clockwork precision. It had to liquidate all second-rate
sectors and to replace them with the intensification of the political, economic, and propaganda sectors of the struggle. Then,
it had to widen its activities over the Eastern Ukraine and to
win the people of the eastern provinces of Ukraine to that struggle. It had also to go out beyond the borders of Ukraine and to
summon others of the subjugated peoples especially in the "satellite" countries, to the struggle against the Bolshevist occupants,
showing them the Ukrainian experience in this uneven fight. We
are able to see that the Ukrainian Resistance Movement has done
this work splendidly.

The Ukrainian Resistance Movement reorganized its forces according to the principles mentioned above in the second half of
1946. Preparations for this reorganisation were made as early as
1945 soon after the war's end, as we can see it from the "Instructions of the Central Directing Body of the OUN in connection
with the conclusion of World War II". The large insurgent units
(battalions and companies) were disbanded and their fighters were
used to strengthen the units of the territorial network. Instead
of disorganized units, small units of armed Ukrainian insurgents
were organized, each with its own area of activity to which it
was confined except in rare cases this was necessary. The detachments were divided into "sub-detachments" and all had their numbers and names. The dislocation of the detachments and subdetachments was planned by the Supreme Command in such manner that they
could easily be mobilized for special actions in case of emergency. At the same, the mobilization order to the affiliated "Youth
Organization" was issued, and young boys and girls between 16-18
years of age joined the armed detachments to complete them to
full strength, and also to get their training both political-ideological and military. At last the Propaganda and Information
Center had been organized, and its chief job was to reorganize the
material base for the continuation of propaganda activities. All
over the Western Ukraine, the armed groups of Ukrainian insurgents
had a difficult task to acquire all kind of typing materials
wherever it was possible. Some of them suceeded in capturing valuable material which was **brought by** underground channels to the
Propaganda and Information Center.

It is clear that the Soviets were to be much surprised at the
vitality of the Ukrainian Resistance Movement, in the second half
of 1946. Having publicly announced their "total" victory over the
UPA, they were dismayed at the reactivating of its forces. Their
disappointment was complete when they learned that there had appeared clandestinely p r i n t e d magazines of the Ukrainian
Resistance Movement with articles by well-known underground **writ**ers such as Poltava, Harnovy, Kuhil, Honcharuk and many others.

Having destroyed the chief base of the Ukrainian underground propaganda during the time of the Ryassny-Moskalenko offensive, they could hardly expect such a regeneration in so short a time. As a matter of fact there had appeared the clandestine magazine of the Supreme Ukrainian Liberation Council, "The Independence", the ideological magazine of the OUN, "Idea and Action" (No.10) and many others as well as thousands of leaflets which found their way all over the Soviet-Union.

The first issue of "The Independence" (1946) contained an excellent article entitled "Shame of the Twentieth Century" which decribed the Bolshevist methods of combatting the Ukrainian Resistance Movement during the time of the Ryassny-Moskalenko offensive. Issue No.10, 1946 of "Idea and Action" contained many interesting articles, among which was one by Poltava, the leading underground writer, entitled "The Ideological Principles of Ukrainian Nationalism".

In the fall of 1946, the Ukrainian Resistance Movement began to fight the forced collectivization of agriculture, as practised in the Western Ukraine, and this became its principal activity in Ukraine during the following years.

To this day in the West, there persists the belief that the collectivization of agriculture, as practised in the Soviet-Union, despite the inhuman methods used for its enforcement, is an economical measure calculated to increase production. Actually, however, in the Western Ukraine and other subjugated countries, collectivization is a p o l i t i c a l action, and is enforced in spite of the fact that it is ruinous economically. Lenin himself has said that if the peasants are allowed to keep their land, they will continue endlessly to produce capitalist elements who, from the countryside, will penetrate into the towns, trade, industry and the administration. In short the existence of a peasant class based on private property, enables capitalism to reproduce itself perpetually making Communism impossible in the long run.

In order to ensure the existence of their regime, the Communists instituted collectivization of agriculture. Needless to say, they met with a desperate resistance on the part of the peasants, especially in Ukraine and in the Cossack lands. Soviet terrorism triumphed, however, and over 30 million peasants, either perished in the Soviet sponsored famine of 1932/33, or were deported to forced labor in the Arctic regions.

The collectivization of Ukraine's agriculture proved most eloquently and conclusively that the kolkhozes were nothing to boast of with regard to productivity of labor, or economy of production. The Bolshevik system needed the kolkhozes only in order to ruin the individual farmers as a class. As is wellknown, the farmers all over the world are the staunchest patriots and the most stubborn fighters for individual freedom and private initiative. Only by means of kolkhozes was it possible to reduce the Ukrainian farmers to the level of slave-laborers, and their real income to the level demanded by the exploitation current in the Soviet Union.

Immediately after the re-occupation of the Western Ukraine the Soviets were making haste to prepare the ground for collectivization. Their success was almost nil, for the Ukrainian Resistance Movement frustrated all their attempts. The Soviets were, therefore, eager to make the Western Ukraine ripe for collectivization. They decided that the best method to achieve this end, was to make the life of the individual farmers as intolerable as possible. These measures were calculated to ruin the farmers and to make them willing to abandon their land. All the farmers who were not partisans of the new order were declared "kulaks" and "enemies of the people" and burdened with exorbitant taxes and deportation and imprisonment threatened if they were not paid. The individual farmers had to pay an income tax which was 3 to 4 times higher then that which the kolkhoz farmers had to pay on their private incomes. Individual farmers owning horses, moreover, had to pay a heavy tax in order to compel them to sell the animals sooner or later. The kolkhozes, however, pay no taxes at all in their first years.

The individual farmers are, moreover, burdened with oppressive statute labor. They must cut lumber, cart fire-wood and timber out of the forests, mend roads and do public transport service. The farmers failing to comply with all these obligations risk the sentence to hard labor coupled with the confiscation of all their property.

The individual farmers must deliver to the state a certain amount of various products every year: grain, hay, milk, meat, wool, potatoes, flax, sugar beets, etc. The state pays ridiculously low prices for these products. But fodder and fertlizers, on the other hand, are reserved exclusively for the kolkhozes.

It is evident that under these circumstances to be an individual farmer in the USSR is far from pleasant. Under these conditions the individual farmers have only one choice if they wish to avoid the deportation to Siberia. This choice is to join a kolkhoz "of their own will".

As long as the Ukrainian Resistance Movement continues strong, will the realization of the Soviet program continue to meet the greatest difficulties. The Ukrainian insurgents, although they come from every class of the population, a great proportion are the sons of farmers, enjoy the complete and unstinted support of the whole Ukrainian peasantry in combatting the hated and unpopular kolkhoz-system.

Owing to the vigorous resistance, the Soviets risked their first venture in collectivization only as late as the fall of 1946, when they thought the Ukrainian Resistance Movement had already been destroyed by means of the Ryassny-Moskalenko offensive. They organized some 50 kolkhozes in the Western Ukraine and provided them with an armed guard from the NKVD troops.

Summoned by the Ukrainian Resistance Movement, the farmers all over the country reacted to the rumors of imminent collectivization with large scale sabotages. They were selling their livestock keeping only one cow each. Grain was being hidden in the woods and pigsties were erected in the most unlikely places as was done during the German occupation. The farmers hid their animals or slaughtered them clandestinely.

Counter-propaganda against collectivization brought on riots in various parts of the country. The existing tractors were demolished on all these occasions for fear of subsequent collectivization. In various places the Communists agitating for collectivization among the farmers were either assassinated or illtreated.

The Ukrainian Resistance Movement did not confine itself to the distributing of many leaflets among the farmers explaining the consequence of their joining the kolkhozes. One night, in Nov., 1946, armed groups of Ukrainians insurgents suddenly attacked the MTS (agricultural machinery stations) - the backbone of the kolkhoz system, and demolished them. Again they attacked the kolkhoz estates and burned them. Both these attacks were made simultaneously in the whole country and the Soviets got a hard blow frustrating their attempts to collectivize farming in the Western Ukraine.

Of course, the Soviets did not give up their efforts to enforce collectivization. In spring, 1947, they organized new kolkhozes and brought more armed guards from the MVD-MGB troops. But the struggle against forced collectivization lasted the whole year and the Soviets could not boast of great success. Even now, in 1949, the Kyiv radio broadcast the following figures from a report of the Secretary General of the Ukrainian Communist Party, N.S.Khrushchev, on the progress of agricultural collectivization in the West-Ukrainian provinces: Volhynia - 80% of collectivized land, Drohobych - 79%, Ternopil - 34%, Lviv - 34% and Stanislav 17%. By his report Khrushchev has indirectly confirmed the success of the Ukrainian Resistance Movement in vigorously opposing the collectivization. We must not forget, in this place, that many kolkhozes of Khrushchev's report exist only on paper, inasmuch as the Soviets are masters in exaggerating their "Successes".

The Soviets have soon realized that as long the Ukrainian Resistance Movement exists, their drive for enforced collectivization will not succeed. They began, therefore, studying the Ukrainian Resistance Movement in order to find out the best measures for combatting it. A center aiming at the liquidation of the Ukrainian Resistance Movement was organized under the jurisdiction of the Ministry of the State Security (MGB). It is significant that this "internal" Soviet-Ukrainian problem was put under the control of an all-union authority in Moscow, and this is one proof more that the Ukrainian Resistance Movement had become a "grave danger".

The anti-collectivization struggle of the Ukrainian Resistance Movement in 1917, gave it a big chance to spread all over Ukraine. In Eastern Ukraine, climatic conditions were unfavorable to crops both in 1946 and in 1917. The meager harvest of 1946 combined with the usual requisitions of grain and other foodstuffs, caused widespread starvation among the Ukrainian kolkhozniks of Eastern Ukraine. On the contrary, climatic conditions in Western Ukraine were extraordinarily good and the harvest there was above average. In the Spring and Summer of 1947, the Western Ukraine was, therefore, crowded with groups of starved kolkhozniks from as far as Kharkiv province and Voronezh province who had been attracted by rumors that the Western Ukraine abounded in food and other goods. As the peasant in the U.S.S.R. lives mainly on the proceeds of his little private garden lot of 0,25-1 hectars, the crowds of the kolkhozniks came into the Western Ukraine to beg for grain and other foodstuffs. The Soviets persecuted them in all possible ways, but their drive to the Western Ukraine was unchecked. It is estimated that more than 1 million kolkhozniks visited the Western Ukraine, taking away at least 200.000 quintals of grain and other foodstuffs.

This was a big opportunity for the Ukrainian Resistance Movement. It issued a proclamation to the "Brethren of the Eastern Ukraine" asking them, "whether they know why they are starving although they are the owners of the richest soil in the world." The proclamation explained the aims of the Ukrainian Resistance Movement and called the Ukrainian kolkhozniks to the common struggle against the Bolsheviks. It stressed that the West-Ukrainians have plenty of food and other goods because they systematically oppose the kolkhoz-system and fight against Bolshevism as the most ruthless exploiter of the Ukrainian people. It asked the kolkhozniks of the Eastern Ukraine to follow their example and to fight against the barbarous Bolshevist system, for an independent Ukraine. It is evident that this leaflet-propaganda was not the only measure taken to influence the guests from the Eastern Ukraine. The West-Ukrainian population was asked to aid the brethren of the Eastern Ukraine in all possible way and to assist them at every step. The slogan: "A Quarter of Grain to the Starving Brethren from the East!" was stuck up everywhere and, besides, the Ukrainian insurgents often held meetings with the kolkhozniks to explain to them the hypocrisy of the Bolshevist system and to advise them how to fight it at home. The success of this propaganda can be judged from the press statements from the Eastern Ukraine showing how the kolkhozniks became passive resisters against the Bolshevist system, hiding foodstuffs and sabotaging the orders of the Communist party. Of course the rumors about the Ukrainian armed resistance in the Western Ukraine spread throughout the Soviet-Union.

In the fall of 1947, the Ukrainian Resistance Movement started an important school action. In the civilized world the mission of schools is to supply the pupils with a certain amount of objective information and to teach them to observe the phenomena of life impartially and objectively. Not so with the Soviet school. The first and paramount mission of the Soviet school is to produce loyal Communists. "The task of the Soviet school is to foster in the pupils a love for our social and political system which is infinitely more perfect than all previous systems," wrote A. Voznesenski, the Minister for Education, in "Pravda", Nov. 17, 1948. "This task cannot be carried out otherwise than in connection with the teaching of all subjects."

It is an open question whether the teachers in the West are fully able to envisage what their colleagues behind the "Iron Curtain" must feel when forced to teach their trusting pupils arrant lies, and an ideology of hate. The latest directives from Moscow require, for instance, that Russian culture and Russian achievements be regarded as the first and oldest in the world and that Western culture be regarded only as a derivative of the Russian one. The origin of the Ukrainian state must be explained "from the point of view of present Soviet historiography", i. e. intentionally falsified. In the same way in all courses in Ukrainian literature and history, it is necessary to emphasize the national peculiarity, originality and greatness of Russian thinkers, writers and scholars and their great influence on the Ukrainian people. The pupils must be acquainted with the Soviet system and convinced of its immeasurable superiority to the bourgeois ways. All this the Ukrainian teachers are compelled to inculcate in the defenseless children, contrary to their own better knowledge that Ukrainian culture was already highly developed at a time when Russia was still a vast woods, peopled by wandering tribes of nomadic barbarians. However, the task of the unhappy teachers are not confined to teaching in the schools. They must "enlighteners of the people" in the broadest sense. In school and out of school the teacher has to be not only a champion of Communism but an active fighter against his own people, Western culture, etc. "The sacred duty of the Soviet teacher is to be the engineer of the growing mind, to combat the efforts of the drugs of capitalism, political neutrality, ideo-logical slackness, bourgeois objectivism, bourgeois Ukrainian nationalism, and religious relics to poison the mind of our youth," wrote a Ukrainian school dignitary. Everything Western is poisonous and degenerate, everything Eastern vigorous and excellent. Every day and every hour the consciousness of the power of the Soviet state must be drummed into the minds of the young people. Not for a minute may the words of Lenin be forgotten that "a school outside of life and politics is a lie and a hypocrisy."

In order to oppose the danger of such an "education" for young Ukrainian people, the Ukrainian Resistance Movement decided to start its own school action. It issued directives to the Ukrainian teachers requiring that Ukrainian culture and its achievements be regarded as the principal aim of education. The detailed instructions of the Ukrainian Resistance Movement asked the teachers to teach Ukrainian literature, Ukrainian history, and geography from the point of view of Ukrainian nationalism. They forbade any anti-religious activity in the school, as Ukrainian religious feelings are predominant in every-day life. The pupils had to be acquainted with the achievements of Western culture and the relation of Ukrainian culture with Western culture had to be stressed. Finally, the pupils had to know what is meant by Soviet exploitation, what the situation of the peasant and workers in the USSR is as compared with that in capitalistic countries, and what the essence of Russian imperialism is. Simultaneously with the directives to the Ukrainian teachers, the Ukrainian Resistance Movement issued a prolamation to the young Ukrainian people asking them to facilitate the difficult task of their teachers.

In connection with this it is interesting to note that as early as 1945 almost 6000 teachers were brought by the Soviets from Eastern into the Western Ukraine with the aim of liquidating the nationalistic tendencies in the teaching of history and literature, and of heightening the standard of ideological and political training. The West-Ukrainian teachers were said to be under the influence of Ukrainian nationalism. Most of the arriving teachers were young girls, often members of Komsomol (Communist Youth organization) and they were, without doubt, under the strong influence of Bolshevist propaganda denouncing the Ukrainian insurgents as "bandits", "murderers", "fascists" and the like. The fear of the "Ukrainian-German nationalists" was so great that the girls refused to take food and to speak to the people in the villages of the Western Ukraine. But the Soviets could not secure satisfactory living conditions for them. The lodgings assigned to them were insufficient and out of repair, food was short and of inferior quality and they had no money to have their clothes and shoes repaired. As they got salaries from 130 to 240 roubles a month, they were not able to buy anything at a time when 1 kg of butter on the black market cost nearly 300 roubles.

The Ukrainian Resistance Movement soon made use of the chance their arrival gave them to spread its ideas among the Eastern Ukrainian population, and to make these teachers factors in a planned fight for Ukrainian independence all over Ukraine. It ordered its members and sympathizers to observe the girls in their every-day lives and to support with food and clothing those who, without any doubt, were good Ukrainians. Moreover, it ordered its members propagandize those girls with ideas of Ukrainian nationalism. The girls had a chance to see at close hand the Ukrainian insurgents in their fight against the Soviets and observe the fanatic heroism of the Ukrainian boys and girls fighting against the Soviets. Soon they became acquainted with the aims of the Ukrainian Resistance Movement and understood the situation as it developed in the Western Ukraine. In many cases they became enthusiastic followers of the Ukrainian Resistance Movement and contributed much to the spreading of its ideas in the Eastern Ukraine. According to the reports from the country, 75% of them are following the directives of the Ukrainian Resistance Movement as regards the teaching in the schools. Many have been arrested and deported by the Soviets, and others have become active fighters for the Ukrainian cause. In November, 1948, one of the girl-teachers, a former Komsomol member from the Eastern Ukraine, Tamara Lutsenko, was killed in the streets of a Sub-carpathian town while executing an order of the Ukrainian Resistance Movement aiming at the assassination of an agent-provocateur. She mortally wounded him, but in his last spasm he succeded in shooting her down with his Sub-MG.

Simultaneously with its school action, the Ukrainian Resistance Movement opposed the conscription of Ukrainian youth into FZU schools which are the most ruthless slave labor for minors. FZU schools are chiefly located in Russia. The minors are uniformed and are subject to a strong, military discipline. They attend schools which are, in fact, the factories producing war material.

Among other, the Ukrainian Resistance Movement carries out a strong propaganda campaign among the veterans of the war. In many of the towns in the Western Ukraine and in the whole of the Soviet Union disabled war veterans can be seen sitting and begging at every other street corner. Those who have lost both legs propel themselves in boxes which move not on wheels, but on old discarded ball bearings. These people always wear their orders and medals and abuse the government openly. The Ukrainian Resistance Movement issued a special leaflet directed to them in order to strengthen their anti-Soviet feelings and it considers them a significant factor in the anti-Bolshevist struggle of the Ukrainian people.

Among the chief activities of the Ukrainian Resistance Movement were the UPA raids in Eastern and Central Europe. The operations of the UPA in the territories of Central Europe have echoed in the press of Western Europe and that of the United States, because many foreign correspondents in Czechoslovakia or in Poland indirectly reported on them.

The first raids of the UPA in Central Europe began as early as 1945. In the Summer of 1945, UPA-forces made extensive propaganda raids into the territory of Carpatho-Ukraine, Hungary, Rumania, Slovakia, Byelorussia, and Lithuania. The success of these operations was great. They had excellent propaganda results for the fight against the Bolsheviks, fostered the opposition against them, and consolidated the population for the fight against the common foe. At the same time they showed the true fighting spirit of the military personnel waging war for an Independent Ukrainian State.

UPA raids into Slovakia became especially notorious. In their march through Eastern Slovakia, the Ukrainian insurgents crossed the districts Stropkov, Oiraltovce, Presov, Sabinov, Bardyjov, Snina and Humenne. In all settlements where they passed, they called together the local population and arranged discussion evenings about current topics. They distributed leaflets in Slovak language and registered a considerable number of volunteers who wished to join the UPA-forces.

On August 28, 1945, in the village of Dispalovce, the commander of the raiding group, 1st Lt. Andrienko, split the raiding group into three parts after having received instructions from the home country. One part of the raiding group went into Carpatho-Ukraine, the other into south-eastern Poland, and the third group, under 2nd Lt. Myron, turned south.

When this group approached Presov, and was on the move near the mountain Simonka (1005 m), the Czech authorities brought in heavy concentrations to surround the woods. All the roads were full of moving troops, heavy equipment and dispatchers. But in spite of all this, the raiders peacefully passed through the villages: Cerbenice, Huviz and Lysecek towards the West. In many villages the Ukrainian insurgents (they were members of the First Insurgent Officer School and mostly students of universities or of high schools) gave vocal concerts. They took leave of the hospitable Slovak territory by giving evening of dancing which was well attended by the local population in Tspelovce, 8 km from the Slovak Polish boundary.

UPA raids deep into Slovakian territory in Spring of 1946 became world famous. This raid was well prepared. Participating troops were aware of the importance of this operation. The raid was preceded by a sudden attack of the Insurgent battailon of Cpt. Didyk on the railway station and town of Lukiv in south-eastern Poland. The Polish garrison fled in panic into the Slovak territory and was disarmed and interned by the Czechoslovak authorities. The fact became known all over the world and the correspondents of different Anglo-Saxon press organs went on the spot to gather reliable information. The first reports on the UPA appeared in the world press. The UPA was described by these correspondents as a force of 20,000 Ukrainians fighting against Red Army detachments, well clothed and armed, well fed and wearing national insignia on their caps. Further information on it was added by Homer Biggart, a New York Herald Tribune reporter, in an April 18, 1946 dispatch. He detailed the UPA activities and stressed the fact that the insurgents behave well toward the civilian populace, and leave churches unscathed even when they have to destroy whole villages. He pointed out that because they strive for an independent Ukraine they are both anti-Russian and anti-Polish.

The raid of the UPA in Slovakia, in Spring and Summer of 1946, was one march of triumph. Everywhere the raiders met with enthusiasm and the Slovaks were delighted that the pay-off for their local Communist bosses had become a reality. The raiding detachments passed the Ukrainian-Slovak boundary in complete secrecy so as not to alert Polish and Czechoslovakian forces. Abundant literature was distributed in this raid which embraced nearly all the districts of Eastern Slovakia.

Another battle of the UPA developed in Slovakia in the Spring and summer of 1947. In May 1947, the Czechoslovakian government proclaimed a state of war emergency in entire Slovakia. As in a time of war people were forbidden to move freely between populated areas. In the evening one was not allowed to leave one's house. The military detachments of the Slovaks which had been sent against the UPA went over to the side of the Ukrainians without offering any battle. Young people began to join the ranks of the UPA. A detachment of the UPA forced out of Slovakia by the Czech armed forces, retreated in separate fragments across Moravia and Czechia. Small groups of Ukrainian Insurgents appeared in the Sadzava woods. The route of some detachments of the UPA led obviously towards Bavaria where they expected to surrender their arms to the Americans. Some of them even crossed the Danube south of lake Balaton in Hungary and reached the Yugoslav territory to join "chetniks" and "kursari".

The same story was repeated in spring and summer, 1948. The Czechoslovakian ministries for war and for interior had published a joint communique which said: "Czech army and police troops are fighting heavily against UPA units who hold position and fortifications of World War II. in Slovakia." It goes on to say that after several days fighting, police troops had taken a bunker whose defenders (three UPA soldiers and a Red Cross nurse) had fought to their last breath with daggers and bayonets after they had exhausted their ammunition.

The battle of the UPA on the territory of Slovakia reveberated several times in the Czech parliament. During the first phase of the UPA raid, in 1947, the Czech Vice-Minister of Military Affairs, Gen. Ferencik, gave the names of the detachments of the UPA and explained to the members of Parliament the political background of the UPA. During the second phase of the raid which took place on the territory of Czechia itself, the Minister of Military Affairs, Gen. Svoboda, addressed the Parliament regarding the battles with the UPA detachments. He gave the exact number of casualties on both the Ukrainian and Czech sides, and described the UPA as "an excellently trained and perfectly organized military force. Its armed equipment was good", he said.

"Tworba", the organ of the Communist Party in Czechoslovakia, wrote in June, 1948, that "small but exceedingly well-equipped and well-disciplined UPA units have again broken into Czechoslovakia", and that it is "most alarming that numerous Czech and Slovak rebels have joined them and begun to liquidate Communists and People's Democrats." It sharply reproached the Soviet-Polish-Czech high command in Slovakia for its failure to liquidate the UPA which, "by its activities, is said to have turned the military forces of the above mentioned three powers into a laughing stock. The very existence of the UPA is encouraging the anti-communist elements in all the East-European countries." "Tworba" blamed the united high command for failing to issue constructive slogans to counteract the ideas of the UPA and command the sympathies of the Czechs and Slovaks.

An echo of the UPA raids in Czechoslovakia was the trial of the members of the UPA which took place in the capital of Slovakia - Bratislava. Beginning on November 19, it ended on November 29, 1948, with the death sentence for the four Ukrainian defendants. On the first day of the trial the presiding judge, Dr. Karol Berdna began to refer to the defendants as "bandits" and "killers". To the astonishment of the court, Ivan Klisch, one of the defendants, rose to protest immediately after the reading of the charges. "We are soldiers of the Ukrainian Insurgent Army," the defendant declared, "As such, we swore to obey the orders of the command of our armed forces; therefore, we strongly protest the court's reference to us as "bandits" and "killers". He went on to demand that they should be referred to as "soldiers of the Ukrainian Insurgent Army," and stated that if their army uniforms and insignia were not returned, they would not answer the questions put by the court. The defiant attitude of the defendants in spite of their long struggle against both the Nazis and the Bolshevists, and the tortures they suffered in the communist prisons of Czechoslovakia, appeared to nonplus the court. A recess was called and after several hours of deliberation the court ruled that their uniforms be returned. For the remainder of the proceedings, the Ukrainian underground was referred to as the Ukrainian Insurgent Army. The trial was much publicized in the Chechoslovak press.

Details of the UPA raids in the Eastern Ukraine are known from firsthand reports by participants in these raids. The first raid under the command of Col. Kney of the UPA-North was organized in Autumn, 1946. It started in Northern Volhynia, which is the operation base of the UPA-North, and finished near the River Dnieper in the region of Kyiv. The raiding group traveled more than 400 kilometres and had 21 encounters on the way. It was divided into small raiding detachments which worked simultaneously executing the orders of their commander as his staff. While raiding in Eastern Ukraine the raiding units often changed their field of operations in order to carry out a given task, to secure supplies, or to evade discovery and prevent encirclement. Strict discipline on the march was maintained. Marches were generally at night, by routes known only to the local population. Small insurgent units synchronized their moves over a large terrain marching 30-45 miles daily. Everywhere the raiding units found the full support of the eastern Ukrainian population which supplied them with food and gave them shelter.

Another raid under the command of Major Khmara was organized in the spring of 1947. It was organized by the UPA-South. The raiding detachments crossed Bukovina, Moldavia, Bessarabia and reached Odessa. The raid covered more than 1000 kilometers and was made in about 100 days. The raiding detachment made connections with many local insurgent groups in Moldavia and Bessarabia and got the full support of the villagers who were glad that the raiding detachment demolished the granaries and distributed grain among the population.

As early as 1945, the UPA made several raids in Poland. It made connection with WIN (Freedom and Independence), a Polish underground army in Central Poland, and with NSZ (National Armed Forces), a Polish underground army in Western Poland. The Ukrainian insurgents went as far as Wroclaw (Breslau) and established liaison with WRN (Liberty, Equality, Independence), another Polish underground organization. The Ukrainian insurgents established not only contacts with the Polish underground, but also concluded an agreement of mutual support and assistance. According to this agreement, which was concluded on May 18, 1946, the combined Polish-Ukrainian underground forces attacked the town of Hrubieszow, on May 27/28, 1946, causing heavy casualties to the NKVD troops and Polish militia.

With the assistance of the Polish underground, the Ukrainian insurgents raided the Bialowieza wilderness (1945, the battailon of "Wolves" under the command of Major Chernyk), and Central and Western Poland (1946), and eastern Prussia (1947 - detachment under the command of Cpt. Prirva). The enforced colonization of East Prussia, mainly with the Ukrainians from the Ukrainian territories West of the Curzon Line provided the UPA with an opportunity to extend its activities to the Baltic Sea and to make connections with the well-organized and strong Lithuanian Liberation Movement. The aim of the last raid was to visit the Ukrainian population in Eastern Prussia, to organize an underground network covering this province and the Danzig area and to establish contacts with the Lithuanian Resistance Movement (BDPS -

National Democratic Resistance Movement). The contacts were established and the Ukrainian insurgents could learn the strength and the perfect underground organization of BDPS.

At the same time the West group of the UPA was concentrating all its efforts on preventing the Red Polish government from forcibly transferring the Ukrainian population from the territories West of the Curzon Line into the Soviet-Union. In accordance with the Soviet-Polish Treaty of August 16, 1945, the Polish-Soviet state boundary was established. The Red Polish authorities announced officially that all Ukrainians had to leave Poland and move to the Soviet-Union. It must be emphasized that this transfer action was carried on by the Red Poles with great terror and violence. The Red Polish Security troops (UB) and the Red Polish Army under Soviet command, destroyed whole Ukrainian villages, setting fire to them, plundering, and murdering the inhabitants. On January, 24, 1946, at 9,00 A.M. units of the Red Polish Army surrounded the village of ZAWADKA MOROCHIWSKA. These units were from the first battalion of the 34th regiment stationed in Sanok. The HQ of the regiment under the command of Col. Pluto, was in the village of Mokre. The Red Polish soldiers murdered 56 persons who were in the village and set fire to the buildings. The soldiers committed many atrocities, torturing their victims before killing them. Not even children and infants were spared, nor did the aged escape a fearful fate. Stomachs of the children were cut open, and their eyes pierced, and women suffered the loss of their breasts and tongues which were cut off by the sadists. Several persons were thrown into flames. The whole village was completely plundered. The Red Polish troops seized 17 horses, 34 cows, and other stock. On March 28, 1946, the same village was again seized by the same battalion of the Red Polish Army. The battalion commander addressed the people gathered in the village square near the schoolhouse, and declared that he would have everyone shot who refused to leave for the USSR. Then he chose 11 men and ordered them to be shot before the eyes of the crowd. The third assault on the same village was made on April 13, 1946, and further inhabitants were shot while fleeing to the woods. Finally, on April 30, 1946 the whole population of this village was forcibly evicted and brought to the railway station at Zahiria to be transported to the USSR. Such was the sad story of one Ukrainian village in this area, and such was the story of many other villages West of the Curzon Line.

It is evident that the UPA was forced to stand in defence of murdered and plundered people. Reinforcements came from Ukraine and the fighting became fierce in this area. On March 28, 1947, one of the leading Red Polish generals, Vice-Minister of War, Gen.Walter-Swiersczewski fell in the fight with the Ukrainian insurgents. He inspected the Red Polish troops in the area of the Soviet-Polish frontier and was killed from the ambush near the town of Baligrod. The assassination of Gen.Swierszczewski was an indication that the activities of the UPA had increased to such proportion that they began to be dangerous to the Soviet-Union and its satellites.

In this place it is important to note that Gen.Walter-Swierszczewski was the fourth prominent enemy leader killed in the fight with the UPA. The first was SA commander LUTZE, the second was Soviet Marshall VATUTIN who was mortally wounded by an UPA-ambush in Northern Volhynia, in 1944, and the third was Gen.Col. MOSKALENKO who was killed in 1946.

The assassination forced the Soviet-Union, Poland and Czechoslovakia to conclude a tripartite pact on May 12, 1947, aiming at mutual aid in the destruction of the UPA-West which operated there. Important forces were brought into action against the Ukrainian insurgents, but they could not break the resistance of the UPA. The Supreme Command of the UPA elaborated its own plan and accordingly divided the UPA West into small detachments. The main forces of the UPA-West broke the encirclement and passed into the Ukraine to continue their fight against Communist oppression. Other detachments were ordered to raid Czechoslovakia, Hungary and the Balkans with the purpose of mobilizing the forces of the other subjugated peoples to the common fight against Bolshevism. The complete removal of the Ukrainian population either to the Soviet-Union, or to Eastern Prussia finally forced the rest of the UPA detachments to abandon South-Eastern Poland and to transfer their action to Poland, or Slovakia where they found a sympathetic element among the populations. On the territory West of the Curzon Line there were left only small detachments for special purposes which passed there winter, 1949, and by summer, 1949, forced their way across Poland and Czechoslovakia into the US Zone of Germany.

On the occasion of the 5th Anniversary of the UPA, Gen.Taras CHUPRYNKA, the Commander-in-Chief of the UPA issued an order which we give here in full.

FIGHTERS AND COMMANDERS OF THE UPA! MEMBERS OF THE URM!

Five years have passed since the period when the members of the OUN OSTAP began setting up armed groups for the struggle against the occupiers of Ukraine. These small groups fighting simultaneously against the Nazi-Germans and the Red Partisans have set new standards of a liberating-revolutionary movement - the Ukrainian Insurgent Army (UPA). In a few months this movement spread to the whole of Polessia, Volhynia, Galicia and Pravoberezzha. The year of 1943 as well as the first half of 1944 are marked by the struggle of the UPA on two fronts. On the anti-Nazi front the UPA stopped the mass deportation of the Ukrainians for slave labor in Germany and made impossible the economic plundering of the people. On the anti-Bolshevist front the UPA prevented infiltration of Red partisan units into Ukrainian territory. It was the UPA that in a series of victorious battles has defeated the hordes of the Stalinite Huns that were sweeping in from the North-East to conquer Europe.

By the second half of 1944, all Ukrainian territories had already come under the Bolshevik occupation. The new period of the UPA struggle for the "to be or not to be" of the Ukrainian people, began. The first attempt to annihilate the Ukrainian people by throwing them into the first lines of the imperialistic war, failed. Following the call of the Ukrainian Resistance Movement, under the protection of the UPA, the Ukrainian male population was able to avoid extermination. The occupiers too failed in forcibly deporting the Ukrainian population to the new slave labor projects in the USSR. Watching the political-military successes of the UPA, and the growing sympathy of the Ukrainian population for it, the occupier has not yet dared to carry out the full economic plunder of the population by forcing the farmers into Stalinite collective farms.

The Ukrainian insurgent has, with arms in his hands, protected the Western ranges of the Ukrainian territories against the flood of Polish imperialistic gangs in 1944, and later rose in defence of the population of these ranges. For two years the UPA waged an unequal struggle against the Bolshevists and their Polish hirelings on the Eastern ranges of the Ukrainian territories; and the Ukrainian insurgent remained there even when the last Ukrainian was taken away by force and the whole zone became an uninhabited desert.

Dauntless commanders and fighters of the UPA have written on their banners a series of feats of arms that will be entered in golden letters in the annals of the Ukrainian army. The punishing hand of the fighter of the UPA has reached prominent representatives of the occupiers such as the Chief of Staff of SA Lutze, the C-i-C of the "1st Ukrainian Front" Marshal Vatutin, or Deputy-Minister of War, Gen.Swierszczewski. Repeatedly the units of the UPA stormed the enemy' administration centers, forced their way into the province centers, and in long-range raids ranged in their own and foreign territories. They have harrassed the enemies by ambushes and invasions and prevented them in realizing their plans of exterminating the Ukrainian people. The names of Hrshot-Rizun, Jastrub, Jasen, Storchan, Prut, Konyk, Peremoha, Khrin have spread the glory of the Ukrainian arms beyond the borders of Ukraine.

But in the field of politics, the UPA also achieved great results. Acting on the slogan: "Liberty to peoples, freedom to the individuals" it organized, as early as 1944, national units of Azerbaidjans, Georgians, Turkestans and other peoples subjugated by Moscow, for the struggle to overthrow the Kremlin and to establish independent states of all these nations in the West. On its initiative, the Conference of the Enslaved Nations was called, in November, 1943. On the x/established the Supreme Ukrainian Liberation Council that, since 1944, directs the all-out struggle at home and abroad for the Ukrainian Independent United State. The UPA raids in Poland and in Slovakia filled the ranks with the new allies from among the Poles and Slovaks.

The successes achieved by the UPA have surpassed the goals set for it by the Supreme Ukrainian Liberation Council and the whole Ukrainian nation. These successes have been achieved by the UPA under conditions not experienced by mankind until now.

Fighters and Commanders of the UPA!

You who today fight in the armed units against the Bolsheviks and you who have swelled the ranks of the liberating-revolutionary underground! Be aware that the five years of the heroic struggle of the UPA and of the liberating-revolutionary underground is the most heroic period of Ukrainian history. The history of mankind does not know such an heroic epoch. New Ukrainian generations will be taught about the heroism of the UPA and of the liberating-revolutionary underground. The UPA-fighter, the Ukrainian revolutionary will replace the manly Spartan in the history of mankind. Be, therefore, conscious of the great epoch in which you live and do not put to shame the glory of the Ukrainian insurgent as did not those who already fell in the fight.

On today's festive day of the UPA, proudly look upon the past five years and remember with veneration all those who, by sacrificing their lives, have forged the New Epoch. On today's festive day look with pride at the future that will crown the New liberation War with Victory!

Long live the Supreme Ukrainian Liberation Council!
x/initiative of the UPA all Ukrainian independent parties united and

Eternal Glory to the Heroes who have devoted their lives to Ukraine!

(Signed) Gen. Taras CHUPRYNKA
Commander-in-Chief
Ukrainian Insurgent Army (UPA)

(This order is translated from the Ukrainian original which was reprinted in the pamphlet of the UPA Group "BUG" published in October of 1947. Commander Ostap, mentioned in the order, a leading figure in the Ukrainian Insurgent Army (UPA) was reported killed in November 1948, in a battle with the Soviet MVD troops near Torchyn in the province of Volhynia.)

On September 25, 1947, in order to offset efforts of various Ukrainian political groups abroad claiming a preferred status in the Ukrainian Insurgent Army (UPA) Taras Chuprynka has issued a declaration, published in the Bulletin of the Central Propaganda and Information Center, in which he emphasizes that the UPA is not associated with any political party, although the OUN headed by Stepan Bandera was most active in its formation. Gen. Chuprynka declared that the soldiers of the UPA were soldiers only, and were fighting for the abolition of foreign rule over the Ukrainians. The political arm of the UPA is the Supreme Ukrainian Liberation Council which has a membership of varied political directions.

The last big action of the Ukrainian Resistance Movement in Ukraine, about which we know from the original UPA reports, is the action against large-scale deportations of the Ukrainians which took place in October, 1947, and in March-April, 1949. Deportation is one of the most efficient methods in the practice of genocide by Soviet Russia. It was legally established in February, 1930, at which time the Council of People's Commissars authorized the local soviets to "take all necessary steps in the fight with the kulaks, including the confiscation of their property and their deportation from the region or district". Millions of Ukrainians were affected by this measure. In his lastest book, The Rape of Poland, St. Mikolajczyk estimates the number of Ukrainians deported to the various parts of the Soviet Union at 10,000,000 people.

In order to understand UPA anti-deportation measures, it is necessary to discuss the characteristics of the deportation and its techniques. First of all the people are entered on the deportation lists. Then the villages are surrounded and the people are arrested and taken to the assemble places and to the railway stations where the cattle trains are waiting for them weeks in advance. The people who in various ways avoided the arrest are not troubled any more and are safe until the next deportation. The whole action takes twenty-four hours. No information is given to the deportees about the destination.

Having this in view, the Ukrainian Resistance Movement with all its afiliations realizes the necessity of intensive intelligence work for successful anti-deportation measures. Long before planned deportation systematic observations by security service (SS) are made on railway stations; information is disseminated and exchanged by various affiliations of the Ukrainian Resistance Movement. Besides intensive intelligence work preceding the deportation is carried out by UPA collaborators and informers within the rank and file of Soviet administration.

The Ukrainian Resistance Movement divides the measures to be

adopted against deportation into offensive action and passive defense measures. The tasks of offensive action are as follows:
(a) Demolition of bridges, roads, and railway tracks; (b) Destruction of wire communications, (c) Terrorization of Soviet collaborators and locally recruited Soviet auxiliary personnel, (d) Surprise raids connected with freeing of deportees and ambushing on trains, columns, convoys, assemble and resting places, etc. Passive measures are designed to make the people avoid the deportation by warning the people threatened by deportation and by hiding them in the underground shelters prepared weeks in advance, by giving them shelters in the woods and forests, etc. In June, 1948, the Ukrainian Resistance Movement issued an instruction telling the people how to behave in case of a large-scale deportation.

A report by Hanson W. Baldwin in The New York Times (May 15, 1949) disclosed that two divisions of Soviet troops in Ukraine and two in the Caucasus were aiding local police to combat anti-communist guerillas. From the Ukrainian source we know that the mentioned "guerillas" made raids from mountain and forest hideouts to resist the large-scale deportation which took place in the spring of 1949. It is highly significant that the actions of the Ukrainian insurgents still require military counter-measures by the Soviets.

The activities of the UPA, despite the determined efforts of the Soviet Union and her subservient satellites to liquidate them, are still formidable and strongly detrimental to communism. The UPA is constantly developing new guerilla techniques, its detachments often change their field of operation in order to carry out a given task, to secure supplies, or to evade discovery and prevent encirclements. Strict discipline on the march is maintained. Marches are generally at night, by routes known only to the local population. The insurgents have their bases in heavily wooded areas and from these bases they make their raids and before the Soviets can strike back they have returned to the forest. In these bases they not only have sod and foxholes but deep bunkers have been painstakingly built, 4-10 meters underground, with store-rooms, first aid stations and shelters. Special troops of NvD-MGB have made the greatest efforts to drive the UPA out of these nests, but they have not succeeded. The insurgents have a splendid news and communication system. What happens today somewhere in the country is known tomorrow in the distant headquarters in the forest bases around the Carpathians. The collectives go up in flames with all their supplies and machines and the transports of the deportees are frequently attacked and the labor slaves set free. The Russian secret police is not in complete control, even on its own territory.

The Ukrainian Resistance Movement is entering its seventh year. The goal of the fight remains unchanged: AN INDEPENDENT, UNITED UKRAINE. And the fight is not hopeless, for the Ukrainian people have their valuable allies- the other peoples subjugated by the Soviets. The desparate peoples of Central and Eastern Europe and Asia are fighting not only their own battle; they are fighting Soviet Russia for "liberty to the peoples and freedom to the individual". And they are fighting Soviet Russia more and more implacable enemy of the entire Western civilization!

7. Ukrainians in their struggle for Freedom

The Ukrainian Resistance Movement has manifested itself most markedly and powerfully during and since the last war. The fact that even at this moment there are several armed groups of the Ukrainian Insurgent Army (UPA) operating under Bolshevist domination attests to the determination of the Ukrainian people to fight against all forms of Russian aggression and persecution. The social and economic system imposed upon the freedom-loving Ukrainian people is naturally totally alien and abhorrent to them. Traditionally individualistic by nature and consequently opposed to communism, the Ukrainian has fought that system with all his might and power. Moreover, he rightly sees Bolshevism for what it actually is, just another facet of traditional Russian imperialism. For him freedom from Moscow and freedom from communism are synonymous. And that is why the Soviet rule of terror and intimidation manifests itself most markedly in Ukraine and why the Soviet policy follows closely the line of the old Russian imperialism in regard to Ukraine. Such a "solution" of the Ukrainian problem by the Soviets has considerably inflamed the anti-Russian feeling among the Ukrainians and Soviet abuses and crimes inflicted upon the Ukrainian people have burned into their soul a hatred of the Bolsheviks and have made them irreconcilable enemies of Soviet Russia. The wholehearted support the Ukrainian Insurgent Army (UPA) has received from all classes of the Ukrainian people is the best proof of such an attitude.

Simultaneously with the armed struggle, well organized anti-Soviet action is being conducted in various sectors of life with one prupose: to undermine the Soviet system and its regime. The only way to liberation of the Ukrainian people is the national liberating and anti-bolshevistic r e v o l u t i o n of the whole Ukrainian nation in a common front with other nations enslaved by Bolshevism. This can only be reached by the revolutionary-liberating struggle of the widest popular masses, by the intensification and deepening of the revolutionary process aiming its full-scale development in a national uprising. Three hundred years ago such a revolutionary process among Ukrainian masses led to the victorious uprising of the Ukrainian people against the Polish rule and the Ukrainian Cromwell, - Hetman Bohdan Khmelnitsky was able to establish a Ukrainian Kozak Republic (1648). According to this, the revolutionary process has to saturate all ways of life and to oppose to the hostile goals and efforts of Bolshevism - the ideals and aims of the liberating revolution and its principles of national-political, social-economical and spiritual-cultural freedom of the people and men. This conception of liberty through revolution was represented by the Ukrainian Resistance Movement since the very beginning of its existence and realized without any deviation and consistently under all situations. The basic element in this conception is the stress laid upon the struggle of the w h o l e nation, of its broadest popular masses, and not solely upon its organized forces (OUN - UPA - UHVR) which are only the pioneers and directing force behind the revolutionary process. The degree of ripeness for the national-liberating revolution depends, in the first place, on the degree it is possible to permeate the popular masses with revolutionary sentiments, on the enthusiasm of the masses for the cause of liberation and finally on their willingness to fight actively against the suppressors.

The internal situation of the USSR is influenced by the imminence of the conflict with the Western Bloc and the concrete possibility of a new war. All policy of the Kremlin is bearing the pressure of this central problem, is more and more focused upon it and is directed by its requirements. The preparation for this new war leads to poverty and to an unheard of exploitation of popular masses to extreme limits. On this background the regime steps up its terror and the hatred and anti-Soviet feelings grow from day to day among the enslaved nations.

This dissatisfaction of the people, their extreme hostile attitude to Bolshevism, to the government and to the party as well as to its economical system and totalitarian order has been growing steadily since the end of the last war. Many reasons have brought about this situation. Above all menacious bolshevistic propaganda has lost all influence concerning the statement that all around the USSR common people are suffering awful poverty because the soldiers of the Red Army had the chance to see with their own eyes the true state of things and spread information all over the USSR. Furthermore, the popular masses of the USSR expected that with the end of the war there would come changes, a greater freedom would be allowed and living standard would raise. The bolshevist propaganda during the war, especially the inofficial branch of it, backed up these demands of the people and promised mervellous things. Instead of "changes" there came bitter disappointments. New five year plans, new state loans, new social competitive campaigns, all signs of the preparation of a new war, caused such a hatred of the population that the Soviet citizen does not suppress his feelings any more and it comes very often to open expressions of these anti-Soviet sentiments of popular masses in Ukraine. The expected "evolution" of the regime has bogged down and what resulted was only the privileged position of the party and of the new Soviet aristocracy (generals, writers, engineers, etc) and the worst slavery, subjugation, pauperization and exploitation of the broad popular masses. The communist doctrine has completely lost all credit in the eyes of all those who possess a sound feeling of what is true and still possess some common sense.

On the other hand, however, objective minds studying Russia and the problem of Russian imperialism must rid themselves of the myth that there is a gap between Russian nationalism and communist internationalism. Long before World War II, the synthesis of Russian imperialism and communist internationalism was achieved. The problem before the rulers of the Kremlin was to reconcile the internationalism of the communist dogma and Russian nationalism. They initiated the glorification of the military past and the military heroes of the Russian nation with the purpose "to bring the Russian people in an environment free of servility before all that was foreign and to destroy every vestige of moral dependence of Soviet citizens on the West" and to develop "the high and noble feeling of pride in their fatherland". Today, this glorification of the military is supplemented by the edifying information that all the great inventions, the radio, steam engine, etc. were Russian; by the propagation of all the great material and moral values of the Russian people, achieved despite the foreigners, and by extolling all Russian works in literature, art, music and science. In that self-exaltation, the non-Russian peoples have been lost sight of. By ignoring the latter the Soviet brand of Russian nationalism sets to Russify the non-Russian peoples of the Soviet-Union. This is a tendency "to overcome the national differences of language, culture, customs... to prepare the liquidation of the national republics and regions... to merge all national languages into one common language, i.e. into Russian language." This upsurge of nationalism can be explained on the basis that the Soviet masters may feel that the time is approaching when they shall have to wage the decisive struggle with the West, but whatever is behind it, the world must not forget that millions of the non-Russian peoples in the Soviet-Union are conducting an implacable struggle against it. The non-Russian peoples, such as the Ukrainians, Belorussians, the peoples of the Caucasus and Turkestan as well as the Cossacks and the Tartars of Idel-Ural, not to speak about the Baltic peoples (Estonians, Latvians, Lithuanians who were always ready to resist any form of forcible Russification and always the first to revolt once Russia was engaged in war. Such was the case in the wars of 1904-05, of 1914-1918 and of 1941.

The only way in which the Bolshevist system has been able to combat the inimical solidarity of the non-Russian peoples has been through the uses of unbridled terror campaigns involving unheard of atrocities and a spy system which permeates and honeycombs all levels of life, the whole governmental set up, industry, army, education, even family life and the church. Spies and police agents are evil features of the Soviet state which lends it its satanical strength. The first aim of the fight for national liberation has been to break the Soviet system of terror, as other factors of the Soviet power are only the derivative products and branches of the terror and spying system. To combat the terrorist Soviet system and to change the hatred and passive hostility of the population into an active fight against the oppressors, in short to destroy Bolshevism as the terroristic system, has been the chief aim of the Ukrainian Resistance Movement. Now, after seven years of fighting against Bolshevism we can say that it has had success. The Ukrainian Resistance Movement has overcome the influence of the Bolshevist terror and propaganda and made the Ukrainian masses conscious of their strength. Instead of just hating Bolshevism and waiting for its fall, the Ukrainian people have started fighting it with all their might to accelerate the revolutionary process.

It would be an utter fallacy to suppose that through social slogans alone the Russian people can be stirred to rebellion against their Communist regime. Bolshevism, as a social phenomenon is deeply rooted in the mentality, social structure and the national tradition of the Russian people. Therefore, it is not surprising that within the span of the thirty years of Soviet rule there was no mass resistance by the Russian people against their despotic government. If Mr. Barmine quotes the activities of the Ukrainian Insurgent Army (Saturday Evening Post: In Defense of the Russian people), in order to state a general discontent of the Russian people with its despotic regime, it was only possible because of general lack of knowledge about eastern European affairs prevalent in the United States. Facts are stubborn things and once we rid ourselves of the myth of the homo-geneity of the inhabitants of the Soviet Russian Empire, we clearly see that uprisings against the Soviet regime have been made by non-Russian peoples, notably by Ukrainians, Lithuanians, and by the peoples of the Caucasus and Turkestan, and never by Russians.

Since the last war the dissatisfaction of the Ukrainian people and other enslaved peoples with Bolshevism has intensified on a national scale. The Bolshevist system has become more and more "chauvinistic" and has openly praised the "superiority" of the Russian people, to recall only Stalin's famous toast to the "Russian people" at a Kremlin banquet in May 1945, when he singled out "the Russian people" as the "most outstanding nation of the Soviet Union." The campaign for the Russification of the non-Russian peoples has become more brutal. Bolshevist imperialism has become merely the latest and most virulent form of the Russian imperialism. The last war has shown clearly that Ukraine as well as other non-Russian populations are hostile towards Bolshevism. Having the experience of the last war and preparing for a new one, Bolshevism is openly striving to strengthen the Russian imperialism and seeking popular support. For Ukraine and other non-Russian countries, this means the Russification of all sectors of life: centralization and colonialism in the state-political field and economic relations, slowing down and primitivization of racial cultures, the extinction of all expressions of national diversities, all this carried out mercilessly and without disguise. Such a policy generates great hatred towards the centralistic Moscow among the enslaved races and this hatred is so great that it is self-perpetuating thanks to the Bolsheviks themselves. But this hatred is also the natural breeding ground for the development of struggles for national liberations within the USSR.

Thus, the real goals of the UPA actions in under-Soviet Europe, go *far* beyond the borders of Ukraine. The Soviet totalitarian practices compel enslaved races to fight the Soviet regime in underground organizations, because non-clandestine methods of opposing the Soviet regime in the Soviet reality are unthinkable. This truth was long ago realized by the Ukrainians who have been fighting Bolshevist imperialism for the last thirty years. But this truth is just beginning to be realized by many other enslaved peoples, especially by the "satellite" countries and by the Baltic states. Ukraine, as the champion of the anti-Soviet fight has thus gained many valuable allies behind the "Iron Curtain." The UPA, which during the war called on the peoples of the Soviet Union to fight with arms in their hands both against Hitler and against Stalin, now finds support everywhere behind the "Iron Curtain," in Poland and in Slovakia, in Lithuania and Belorussia, in East Prussia and in the Crimea. Following the historic tradition of Ukrainian revolutionaries it tries to organize a league of peoples oppressed by Soviet tyranny and to form a wide front of national underground armies fighting against Moscow. It is important always to remember that this is a struggle of ideas and that the nationalist movements among the enslaved peoples of the USSR constitute a most dynamic force and, therefore, the idea of national liberation is the most powerful weapon in the hands of these opponents of Soviet Russia. Surprisingly enough the democratic press of the free world has given little - if any - attention to this significant fact.

The International Press Bureau released on Dec.8, 1948, a lengthy article, dealing with the future map of Europe, which, according to the informants of the Bureau, is being charted now by the oppressed peoples of Eastern Europe. The aspirations of many peoples are closely tied to the plans, accredited to General Taras Chuprynka, commander-in-chief of the Ukrainian Insurgent Army (UPA). This plan, which is said to be widely circulated inside the Soviet Union, aims at the transformation of the Soviet empire into a series of national independent states. What is known as the "Chuprynka Plan" is a far-reaching blueprint of the reorganization of Eastern Europe and Asia based on national self-determination of the enslaved peoples within the Soviet Union and the "satellite" states as the first and most important pre-requisite of the "world of tomorrow", "which will be followed by the establishment of four principal state units as follows: (1) Siberia, (2) the Caucasus, (3) Turkestan and (4) the Scandinavian-Black-Sea Unit." The importance of the latter for the "world of tomorrow" cannot be overemphasized. Economically, it would be a precious pearl in the future "United Europe". The cornerstone of the Scandinavian-Black Sea Bloc - Ukraine - is the world's third largest producer of iron, fourth in coal, eighth in oil, and has the largest manganese mines in the world. It is veritable "granary of Europa", and for generations has been a breadbasket for all Europe. And it is in Ukraine that a powerful anti-Soviet underground army, the UPA, is still waging a gallant fight for the realization of these ideas.

8. The Political Program of the Ukrainian Resistance Movement

The history of every people of the world reveals continuous efforts in seeking national self-determination and freedom. Many a bitter battle has been fought to free a given people from encroachment upon its human, economic and political rights by more aggressive and stronger nations. In like manner, at the end of the First World War, the Russian Empire of the Tsars was forced internally by her subjugated peoples to permit the creation of a series of national states on its ruins. In the throes of the civil war, the Russian Revolution, 1917, various disfranchised peoples declared in quick succession their national independence from Russian political domination and oppression. Democratic, free national states of Finland, Estonia, Latvia, Lithuania, Poland, Ukraine, Belorussia, Georgia, Armenia, Azerbaidjan, Siberia and Turkestan, Cossacks of Don and Kuban, Mountaineers of Northern Caucasus, Tartars and Bashkirs of Idel-Ural, declared themselves sovereign states, completely independent from Muscovite Russia. It must be stressed here that during the Revolution the claim for freedom by subjugated and stateless peoples was repeatedly guaranteed and affirmed by the present regime of Soviet Russia.

Thus, nearly thirty years ago, a free Ukrainian state came into being, calling into a free statehood a Slavic nation almost as large as France. This Ukrainian National Republic was recognized de facto by Great Britain and France, and de jure by Germany Austro-Hungary, Bulgaria, Turkey, the Republic of Don Cossacks, the Republic of Kuban Cossacks, the Republic of Northern Caucasian Mountaineers, Belorussia, Georgia, the Russian Soviet Federative Socialist Republic and Poland. When the freedom of this Ukrainian Republic was threatened by the Bolsheviks, the Ukrainian government under Gen. Simon Petlura appealed in vain to the Western democracies for help and Ukraine was forced to sink again under the iron rule of Moscow. The Baltic States, Finland and Poland succeeded, with the aid of the Allies, in retaining their independence, while Ukraine, Belorussia, Georgia and other peoples to the east again lost their independence under the might of Russian aggression and forceful military occupation. As a result, Ukraine, the largest nation without statehood in Europe, along with other smaller subjugated nations of Western Europe became in effect Russian colonies. In many ways the operating methods of Russian colonial rule surpass all the indignities forced upon colonial peoples in the darkest corners of the world.

Again and again during the past thirty years the advocates of the Ukrainian independence and the martyrs for Ukrainian freedom have brought to the world's attention the character of the intruding despotism that has wiped out every phase of Ukrainian liberty, murdered its leaders, starved its peasants by the million, and deported millions of others to die in the Far East and North. To all of this story, the Western world has remained passive, silent and indifferent.

The present Ukraine is historically and ethnically Ukrainian territory, which has been populated, developed and defended for centuries by the Ukrainian people. By all human rights it should belong to the Ukrainian people as their national state. The Ukrainian Resistance Movement is now fighting for the establishment of the Ukrainian Independent State.

As under the German occupation, so today the Ukrainian Resistance Movement under the Soviet regime fights for the national and social freedom of the individual men and of nations. Its watchword is: "Freedom of the Individual, Freedom of Nations!". Ukrainian Resistance Movement fights, therefore, for the destruction of the dungeon - Russia - and for the eventual freedom of all nations now suffering under the Bolshevik yoke. The fight against Bolshevik totalitarianism can be successful only through the amalgamation of the strength and power of all the subjugated peoples. Fighting for the formation of a Ukrainian Sovereign nation on all its ethnographic homeland, Ukrainian Resistance Movement is at the same time fighting for the construction of other free and truly democratic nations now within the boundaries of the USSR. All the nations enslaved by the USSR are in the same circumstances and, therefore, they are all natural allies of the Ukrainian people in this common cause. The circle of natural allies in the Ukrainian fight for freedom automatically widened and strengthened at the end of the Second World War, once the Baltic nations and the "satellite" countries of the Balkans and Central Europe found themselves in the Soviet sphere of influence. Fighting for the establishment of free and democratic states now within the USSR, the Ukrainian Resistance Movement is also fighting for the restitution of sovereignty and independence of the "Satellite" states of the Soviet Union.

Thus, the principal aim of the Ukrainian Resistance Movement is the overthrow of Bolshevism and the establishment of the new order in Central and Eastern Europe and Soviet Asia, based on the principle of self-determination of peoples, on independence and sovereignty of national states within their ethnic borders, and on the idea of social justice and prosperity of the popular masses. The realization of this aim entails: (a) the partition of the USSR into national states established on their ethnic territories; (b) the restitution of national sovereignty to the "vassal" states of the USSR which were deprived of their sovereignty in the course of and after the Second World War. Furthermore, the realization of these aims calls for: (1) complete democratization of state and social life of nations, liberated from Bolshevik yoke, (2) free choice of forms of government and of social and economic structures, (3) assurance of "Four Freedoms" for liberated nations, (4) assurance of free spiritual and cultural development for the peoples in question.

Such a solution alone can settle the rightful demands of all the nations concerned, can bring order to Central Europe and Eastern Europe and Soviet Asia and aid in keeping a lasting peace for the entire world. Otherwise the entire political and economic structure of Europe and the world will again the based on fragile foundations, producing unrest among the peoples and offering invitations to future invaders and "liberators", disrupting the economic and political security of the world and endangering the durability of peace.

Fighting for the elimination of the totalitarian Stalinite government, for the overthrow of Bolshevism, for the extermination of the clique of Stalinite satraps and for the progressive order in the whole of Central and Eastern Europe and Soviet Asia, the Ukrainian Resistance Movement realizes that a just social-economic order covering the interest of the broadest masses of population has a firstrate importance[x] of our times shows that the unstable political order, shaky social-economic system, low living standard of the population undermine the structure of any state and society. Therefore, the Ukrainian Resistance Movement fights for a Ukrainian State without exploiters or exploited, for a full participation of all citizens in civilian liberties and where all efforts of the government will be directed towards the raising of living standards. Economic democracy is clearly envisaged in the political program of the Ukrainian Resistance Movement, the best way to show it, is, to quote one of the proclamations, widely spread all over Ukraine by the Ukrainian Resistance Movement during the campaign against the Soviet elections of 1946.

Here we reproduce it in its entirety translated from Ukrainian.

UKRAINIANS! Away Stalin's imperialist tyranny! UKRAINIANS!
Away Stalin's imperialist tyranny!
Away Stalin's compulsory election!
We will not go to vote for terrorism, plunder, imperialism, slavery and tyranny, for hunger and misery!
We will go to democratic elections in free and Independent Ukrainian State!
UKRAINIANS! We will not go to vote for Stalin and his dictatorial party! We will not go to vote for new Red bourgeoisie, for party exploiters, for the leeches of people's blood!
We will not go to vote for compulsory work for hunger pay, for stakhanovization that wrings sweat and blood from the worker!
We will not go to vote for kolkhozes, for slavish work of the peasants, for the unheard of exploitation and plunder of property, work and blood of the workers and peasants!
We will not go to vote for imprisonments, for concentration camps, for deportations to Siberia, for burning of our villages by savage police NKVD gangs, for maltreatings of the masses, or for the murders perpetrated daily by Stalin's police!
We will not go to vote for Moscow's sway over Ukraine: We will not go to vote for Moscow's sway over Byelorussia, Lithuania, Latvia, Finland, Poland, Rumania, Bulgaria and many other countries of Europe and Asia which have been occupied, by violence, through Red Muscovite imperialism!
We will not go to vote for new imperialist wars which bloody Stalinite imperialists are preparing!
We will not go to vote for those who betrayed and annihilated the ideals of the French Revolution about the rights of man, who betrayed and ruined Christian culture, who have been faithless to any ideals of Socialism!
Away with Bolshevik monopoly dictatorship, totalitarianism and terrorism!
Away with bloody Red Fascism - blood brother of German Nazism!
Long live the freedom of human thought, religion and speech!
Long live freedom of the press, literature, art and science, denied and ravaged by the totalitarian system of bolshevism!
Long live freedom of assembly, freedom of criticism, freedom of political and parliamentary representatives of the peoples. Long live freedom of political, social and professional organizations!
Long live free elections and democratic parliamentary governments, pushed aside and spoiled in the Bolshevik regime!
Long live freedom of work! Long live the right of all workers to the products of their own work! Long live social justice, welfare and happiness for all men!
Long live Independent Sovereign Ukrainian State! Long live Free States of all nations in reciprocal alliance, friendship and fraternity!

x/ for the realization of its aims in future. The historical experience

FREEDOM TO NATIONS! FREEDOM TO THE INDIVIDUAL! DEATH TO TYRANNY!

February, 1946,   Ukrainian Insurgents.

Such is, in short, the political program of the Ukrainian Resistance Movement. In any case, it is certain that a democratic Ukraine will be able to cope more adequately with the problems of social, economic, political and cultural needs for the benefit of her people than could any imaginable nations ruling her by force. And, therefore, the Ukrainian Resistance Movement is fighting with all its might to destroy this force and to free the Ukrainian people from the yoke imposed on them by the foreign invaders.

9. The Territory of Ukraine under the Control of the Ukrainian Resistance Movement

As a result of the Second World War almost all Ukrainian lands came under Soviet rule. Only little strips of Ukrainian territory remained in Poland, Slovakia and Rumania. The Ukrainian territory under Soviet rule comprised in Europe 330.000 sq.m. with a population according to the census of 1939 - 50,000,000. The Ukrainian Soviet Socialist Republic is only the part of Ukraine, ethnographically speaking. It has an area of 22,000 sq.m. with population 40,000,000 (1939). Situated in the southwest of the USSR; bordered on the south by the north coasts of the Black Sea and Azov Sea, on the east by the region which adjoins the Don River, and on the west by the northeastern slopes of the Carpathian Mountains and by the Curzon Line, it merges almost imperceptibily into Russia on the north. Ukraine has a fortile soil, a mild, humid climate and rich mineral desposits such as coal, iron ore, manganese, salts, oil and building materials. During World War II the problem of drawing Ukraine's western frontier arose and was discussed at the Conference of Teheran (November, 1943). At the Crimea (Yalta) Conference (Febr.1945) Roosevelt, Churchill and Stalin agreed that "Poland's eastern frontier should be based on the Curzon Line, with qualifications in her (Poland's) favor. This was a slight sacrifice of territory from the Russian-German (Molotov-Ribbentrop) partition of 1939. As a result, more than 1,000,000 Ukrainians found themselves under Polish rule. On August 16,1945, Russia and Poland signed a boundary agreement in which Russia conceded to Poland modifications of from 3-5 miles east of the Curzon Line in some areas. Another agreement provided for the exchanges of population between Poland and Ukraine.

Ukraine is inhabited by Ukrainians which constitute 80% of the population. The Ukrainian SSR includes Vinhitsa, Volhynia, Voroshilovgrad, Dnipetrovsk, Drohobych, Zaporozhe, Izmail, Kamenets-Podolsk, Kiev, Kirovograd, Lviv, Nikolaev, Odessa, Poltava, Rivne, Stalino, Sumy, Ternopil, Kharkiv, Khersson, Chernyhiv, Chernivtsi, Stanislav, Shitomir and Transcarpathian Provinces.

The Ukrainian Soviet Socialistic Republic, which in the spring of 1945 was formally accepted at the Conference in San Francisco as a member of the United Nations, is theoretically an independent state within the frame of the Soviet Union. Although it is called a separate republic, Ukraine does not enjoy liberty of action, because the most important political, economical, and cultural decisions concerning Ukraine and other constituent Soviet republics as well as so-called "satellite" states are invariably made by the authorities in the central Moscow administration.

As it would be expected, over such a large area as Ukraine one finds a considerable variety of scenary and of climate conditions. Apart from the ramparts of the Carpathians in the west and the Crimean mountains in the south, Ukraine is level country, gently rolling in some provinces. In the east and south there is a predominance of the open steppe type of landscape, reminiscent of many stretches in the Middle West of the United States. Ukraine is poor in forests (12%) and for that reason presents extremely disvantageous conditions for a guerilla warfare, but regions more suitable for such purposes lie in Western Ukraine - the marshy forests of Polessia and of northern Volhynia, north of Kyiv and Zhitomir and in the Carpathian mountains. However, the Carpathian mountains, with their gentle slopes, broad valleys and thin forests cannot be compared with natural fortresses of the Alps, or the like. Forced by Russian Tsarist troops in 1914, and by the Red Army in 1944, the Carpathian mountains do not represent any serious obstacle to a great army. Moreover, these mountains are quite accessible to light troops directed against the guerillas.

Today, the Ukrainian Resistance Movement controls an area of nearly 100,000 sq.mil. comprising a population of more than 15.000,000 inhabitants. In this area the Soviets have been forced to retire leaving strong garrisons in large towns and administrative centers of rayons (subdivision of provinces). The network of the Ukrainian Resistance Movement embraces all the urban and rural places of this territory, having everywhere its resistance groups and armed UPA units in each country. The underground has its own system of administration protected by armed guerillas, its own security service having secret informers in the ranks of the Soviet army and police, and numerous other varieties of resistance cells. It is the area of Polessia (Province of Pinsk - Byelorussian Soviet Socialist Republic), Volhynia (Provinces of Rivne and Volhynia), Subcarpathian area (provinces of Stanislav and Drohobych) and Bukovina (province of Chernivtsi). The Ukrainian Resistance Movement has partly spread over the Carpatho-Ukraine, Galicia (province of Lviv), Podolia (provinces of Ternopil, Kamenets-Podolsky, Vinnitsia) and the province of Zhitomir. Recent news indicates the increase of the UPA activities in the mountains of the Crimea. The woods and forests north of Kyiv and in the district of Chernyhiv are reported to be full of Red Army deserters and other anti-Bolshevik elements. The wilderness of Bialowieza, in the frontier region of Poland, Lithuania, Byelorussia and Ukraine is the spot where more than once the meetings of the guerilla groups of different underground armies have been held. The Ukrainian territories to the west of the Curzon Line were the wide field of the UPA activities up to the middle of 1947.

Persistently the Ukrainian Resistance Movement tries to expand its activities to include all of Eastern Ukraine with its unfavorable terrain for guerilla activities. It must be said that the conditions for the guerilla warfare are extremely unfavorable in this area. The area comprises a belt of steppes, wide expanses of level rolling country, completely deforested, with very sparse population. There, the Ukrainian Resistance Movement has constantly been trying to organise underground resistance cells in the urban industrial places. It succeeded in establishing its groups in this area, because many West Ukrainian youths and girls were recruited to work in Donets coal mines and Zaporozhe iron works. Banishment to forced labor has all too often been the fate of Ukrainians, but this drive at present was a big chance for the Ukrainian Resistance Movement which sent many of its members to this area as labor "volunteers". As a result, the Ukrainian Resistance Movement has built up its strong cells in Stalino, Makeyevka, Dnipopetrovsk, Nikopol, Dniprodzerzhynsk, Zaporozhe, Nikolayev, Kryvyi Rih, Odessa, etc. Along with resistance cells the underground religious communes have been organized in this area and "God's underground" is widely spreading all over Ukraine. Among the local population of this industrial area the Ukrainian Resistance Movement has received whole-hearted support and gained most devoted and enthusiastic followers.

The Ukrainian partisans operating in Ukraine and raiding over the neighboring countries were the only partisans in Europe who did not receive supplies from the air. They could get their arms and ammunition only from their enemies by disarming enemy detachments and by assailing enemy military transports. The only support the Ukrainian partisans have ever had in their fight is the full support of the whole Ukrainian population. This support far exceeds any haphazard type of aid given only from time to time. It is no exaggeration to say that owing to this support, the Ukrainian Resistance Movement has repeatedly been able to survive all the offensives, raids and blockades of the Bolshevists during the large scale actions against UPA since the end of the last war.

10. The Forces of the Ukrainian Resistance Movement and their organization

It would be an utter fallacy to think of the Ukrainian Resistance Movement as if it were only the armed battle groups of the Ukrainian Insurgent Army (UPA). In fact the Ukrainian Resistance Movement consists of diverse units and forms a wide-spread underground organization, based chiefly on the political network of the OUN (Organization of the Ukrainian Nationalists).

The Ukrainian nationalist underground has existed on Ukrainian soil for the last thirty years. In spite of the fact that the Soviets and Nazis referred to OUN as a "fascist" or "terrorist" organization, or even a "subversive movement", because its existence threatened the fruition of their plans, it is only a political and military organization of the Ukrainian patriots who strive for the liberation of Ukraine and for Ukrainian statehood. If it uses "subversive" methods, it is only for the reason that there are no legal methods by which a struggle for independence can be carried on in Russia. As clandestine x/and adopt military procedure within its organization.

The Organization of the Ukrainian Nationalists (OUN) was born long before "fascism" or "hitlerism" has appeared in Europe. OUN's first predecessor was RUP (Revolutionary Ukrainian Party), an underground Ukrainian political organization which was founded by an ardent Ukrainian patriot Mykola Mikhnovsky as early as 1902. We can find its successor in the Ukrainian Military Organization (UVO) which came into being after the fall of the Ukrainian National Republic in 1921. UVO was founded by the officers and soldiers of the Ukrainian army who decided to continue to struggle for independence. Headed by late Col. Evhen Konovalets, a former Ukrainian army corps commander, it gradually changed its character from that of military organization, widened its activities and assumed the form of an illegal political organization. At the First Congress of the Ukrainian Nationalists in Prague in 1929, the Organization of the Ukrainian Nationalists came into being, the successor of the Ukrainian Military Organization (UVO). It was lead by Col. Konovalets until the day of his death in 1938.

Faithful to the motto of OUN: "You will secure the Ukrainian statehood, or die fighting for it", the Ukrainian patriots who joined OUN declared war on the enemies of the Ukrainian independence. It was the OUN which organized the first serious opposition to xx/advancing Hungarian army in Carpatho-Ukraine. In 1941 OUN gave birth to the Ukrainian Insurgent Army (UPA), which in the beginning consisted only of the battle groups of the OUN. As the sole political organization of the Ukrainian people which was

x/organization it must operate with the best principles of conspiracy
xx/Hitler's plans in Eastern Europe. As early as 1939, OUN put up a ste
stern opposition to the

active under the German and Russian occupation of Ukraine, it appealed to the Ukrainian people to join the struggle for independence against the German and Russian occupations. The Ukrainian people followed the call of the OUN and the ranks of the Ukrainian Insurgent Army (UPA) swelled with Ukrainian peasants, workers and intellectuals, who took arms to rid Ukraine of the Germans and Soviets. In this manner the Ukrainian Insurgent Army (UPA) became the armed organization of the whole Ukrainian people.

Since it consisted of true Ukrainian patriots, the OUN in Ukraine never had monoparty tendencies and when, as the result of widening the revolutionary process in Ukraine, the Supreme Ukrainian Liberation Council (UHVR) came into being in 1944, OUN participated in its creation by sending a delegation to the Ukrainian National Congress. OUN subordinated its activities to the direction of the elected Council and General Secretariate of UHVR and follows the directives of it. In the scheme of the Ukrainian Resistance Movement the OUN holds the responsibility for special branches and services of the Ukrainian Resistance Movement and is the unit of the Movement in Ukraine.

Today, besides its political activities, the OUN is the quartermaster of the Ukrainian Resistance Movement responsible for regular delivery of the required supplies to all units of the Ukrainian Resistance Movement at stipulated times and places. It supplies the Ukrainian Resistance Movement not only with money, food, clothing, war material and other supplies, but also with trained men. It is responsible for all communications to headquarters and other units on a similar level. It looks for the necessary contacts between the different units of the Ukrainian Resistance Movement and prepares quarters and underground bunkers for the winter quarters of the resistance fighters as well as underground shelters for special purposes. It supplies combat troops with all the ordnance stores that they may require and recovers and repairs their equipment. It also has the responsibility for provision of laundry service, for decontamination of clothing and for protecting the units and installations of the Ukrainian Resistance Movement from enemy attack. It maintains depots, workshops, ammunition depots and small factories for soap, leather, tanneries, etc. It provides for the transportation of the supplies needed by different units of the Ukrainian Resistance Movement. It is concerned with personnel, which includes recruiting, training (only political and ideological), organization, administration, discipline and welfare.

The political credo of the OUN remains the same as it was during the Nazi occupation. It is fighting for a free and democratic independent Ukrainian state, for the destruction of the Bolshevik exploitation and slave labor system, for the liberation of the Ukrainian peasant, worker and intellectual from political and social-economic slavery, for freedom of the press, of expression, of religion, for free cultural progress unhampered by Stalinite dictatorship, etc. Through its tireless counter-propaganda the OUN explains to the peasants, workers and professional intelligentsia the unbridgeable chasm between the ideals propagated by the Bolsheviks and their application under the existing Soviet conditions. It trains all Ukrainians in anti-Soviet methods and reminds the Ukrainians by propaganda in the underground press and by word of mouth of the nature of Bolshevism and its aims towards Ukraine and toward the rest of the world. It tries to unite all the oppressed peoples of Eastern Europe in a common front against Bolshevism and to prepare them for an all-out anti-Russian and anti-communist uprising when the opportune time arrives.

The widening scope of these activities was possible because the OUN has wide-spread territorial underground organization of its own existing in the country for years. Even today the widely dispersed and well-concealed network of the OUN which closely cooperates with the UPA, embraces the wide territories of Ukraine.

In addition to the territorial organization of the OUN, the Ukrainian Resistance Movement controls such important services as "Security Service" (SB), "Ukrainian Red Cross"(UCK), "Propaganda Service", and "Technical Service" (TZ) which have an autonomy of their own within the frame of the Ukrainian Resistance Movement.

The Security Service of the Ukrainian Resistance Movement (SB) is the most effective service and is composed of the best underground fighters. It is very well organized and has done the Soviets much harm by its activities. It succeeded in organizing a network of its collaborators among the Soviet officials as well as among the Soviet army and police forces. It is the sector of the Ukrainian Resistance Movement which is most hated by the Soviet occupational administration. This is evident in an article entitled "Nationalist Phantoms" published on Aug.14, 1946, in the Soviet-Ukrainian official newspaper "Radyanska Ukraina" (Soviet Ukraine). The author of this article stated frankly that the fight against Ukrainian "nationalists" is very difficult, because the latter are "masters of masquerade", and have a "security service" of their own which consists of the most experienced "bandits". Also they have their own "propaganda" based on the ideology of the publications of Prof.Michael Hrushevsky and Prof.Serhiy Yefremov. These were Ukrainian scholars "liquidated" by the Soviets.

Another statement concerning the Ukrainian SB was included in the "manifesto" of Premier Khrushchov and NKVD general Ryassny to the Ukrainian Insurgents and SB-men. They stated that the "criminal" and "dangerous" SB holds the troops and civilian population in strong discipline. Another statement was included in the secret order of the chief of MGB (political police) of the province of Drohobych (Western Ukraine) General Saburov. He stated that the "SB" is "a very dangerous organization", that it adopted the "hitlerite methods of provocation" and tried "to fight insubordination and desertion with all its forces." Gen.Saburov asked the "constant vigilance" of his subalterns and instructed them as to the "methods of combatting SB activities".

The "Ukrainian Red Cross" is the wide field of women's activities. It provides the medical service in the Ukrainian Resistance Movement. Under its jurisdiction come the various nursing services, the evacuation, care, and treatment of sick or injured reistance fighters, advice on measures to insure the health of troops and population, supply and replenishment of medical equipment, and supply and organization of field ambulances for the Ukrainian Insurgent Army (UPA). It mobilizes the girls and trains them as nurses for the UPA, organizes the underground hospitals and cares for wounded and sick soldiers of the UPA. The underground hospitals of the UPA became famous throughout the world. The Red Polish newspaper "Glos Ludu" (People's Voice) wrote about one of these hospitals in June, 1947: "Recently an underground hospital was discovered in a forest. There was nothing seen on the surface but trees and grass. Ten metres under the ground there was a hospital with corridors, operating rooms, infirmaries, beds and medical equipment. When the hospital had been discovered, the doctors and the nurses defended themselves heroically and committed suicide when the ammunition came to an end." The correspondent of the

Polish Communist newspaper ended his article by saying: "Nobody on the surface heard anything of this underground tragedy of men and women... who showed a ferocious fanaticism and strange heroism." Another description of such a hospital we can find in "Le Phare" (Brussels) in the issue of July 10/11, 1948, and in the "Times" (London) of June 20, 1947. The role of the Jewish doctors must be emphasized here. During the time of the German occupation of Ukraine, the Ukrainian Resistance Movement mobilized many Jewish doctors, pharmacists, and nurses into its service, in this way saving their lives. When the Bolshevists came back to Ukraine, Jewish doctors and nurses continued to serve with the Ukrainian Resistance Movement. Many Jewish doctors and nurses offered their lives in the fight against the Brown and Red occupants of Ukraine. A Jewish doctor called Kum died as a hero in the defense of the field-Hospital which had been under his care for more than two years, in Trukhaniv in the Carpathians (1945). Another Jewish doctor, Maksymovich, committed suicide when facing liquidation of his field-ambulance in the Carpathians.

The Ukrainian Resistance Movement has developed a very good propaganda service of its own. Every detachment of the UPA as well as each unit of the territorial organization, has its own propagandist who is responsible for the propaganda service and propaganda activities in the area where it operates. All those propagandists follow the directives of the "Propaganda Center" which is located somewhere in Ukraine. The "Propaganda Center" has its printing presses where the press organs, periodicals and leaflets are printed. There are many underground periodicals in Ukraine, The leading magazine of the Organization of the Ukrainian Nationalists is "Ideya i Chyn" (Idea and Action). Others are the magazine of the Ukrainian Insurgent Army (UPA) "Povstanets" (The Insurgent), the magazine of the Supreme Ukrainian Liberation Council (UHVR) "Samostiynist" (Independence), the humorous paper "Perets" (The Pepper), the popular information paper "Informacijni Visti" (Information News), "Lisovyk" (The Man of the Forest), etc. It is interesting to note that Ostap Vyshnya, once the outstanding Ukrainian satirist and author of the "Smiles" who was banished to Siberia in the thirties, was brought back in 1945 to Ukraine to combat widespread Ukrainian underground satiric pamphleteering. Because the Ukrainian illegal satiric magazine "Ukrainian Pepper" was very popular in Ukraine, the Soviet government founded in Kiev a magazine called "The Red Pepper", and Vyshnya was put in charge of it. Apparently he did not justify the Communist party hopes, since the Union of Ukrainian Writers, a Soviet official organization, upon the order of the Politbureau, charged that the "Red Pepper" was "substituting spite and vulgarity for popular humor."

The underground propaganda network quickly disseminates all available information by means of the whisper propaganda technique which is much used. In addition letters, newspapers, bulletins, posters slogans, and pamphlets are printed and distributed chiefly in the urban places where military garrisons are stationed. The propaganda in the Soviet army is considered especially important. Material which is small in size and easily distributed is used when the Soviet Army units are busy carrying out round-ups and blockades against the UPA. Slogans like "Do you went to go on starving?", "Do you know what the fight is for?", or "Down with Stalin's tyranny", and the like, have a strong influence upon the morale of the Soviet Army soldiers. The Ukrainian Resistance Movement published thousands of leaflets calling the Soviet army officers and soldiers to the common fight against Stalin's tyranny. It spoke to them with a profound knowledge of the terrible conditions of life under the Soviet regime. "With the overthrow of Hitler," wrote UPA in its proclamation to the Red Army in 1946, "only dictators-imperialists have changed their positions. Nothing has changed in the conditions of the People, of the working masses. Oppression, exploitation, and terror go on." After this statement the UPA summoned: "Your fight for the victory of justice has not ended yet. You will end it, if you overthrow the dictatorial-terroristic exploitation system of the greatest foe of the people, Stalin's government, and his gang of people's exploiters, the Communist Party. Let us undermine the Stalinite system from within..."

A book by Mykola Lebed which has been published in Ukrainian about the origin, growth and activity of the UPA reprints the texts of different appeals which were addressed to the Georgians, Armenians, Cossacks, Volga Tartars, and other non-Russian nationalities. Each text was adapted to the grievances and historical background of the people concerned. Some leaflets were printed in Russian, others were printed in the original language of the people concerned, using even the type faces of the language concerned (Georgian). During raids in Poland or Czechoslovakia, the leaflets in Polish, Czech and Slovak languages were issued by the thousands, summoning the respective peoples to fight against the common oppressors. The appeals conclude: "We shall fight for the Ukrainian independent state and for independent states of all the peoples whom the Bolshevik hangmen have enslaved... The peoples of Europe do not want Hitlerism or Stalinism... Long live the revolution of the oppressed peoples! Long live the sovereign states of all peoples! Long live peace and friendship of peoples!"

There are different methods of distributing propaganda material. In the urban places, the small size propaganda material is put into letter boxes at the door, or into coats or other garments in the restaurants and cafes, and into books and magazines in public libraries . Other small size material is sent by post. In some cases Soviet officials are taken prisoners and then set free after being given intensive orientation and having been provided with propaganda literature. Other persons from the Soviet administration are selected and the individual approach is organized. In some cases meetings for the population are organized, and different points of the Soviet propaganda line is attacked. Theater performances and concerts for the Ukrainian population were organized by a special propaganda group called "Flying Estrade" under the protection of the UPA.

Revolutionary formations of the UPA and OUN pay very great attention to the fight in the economical sector. Everywhere in Ukraine slogans against Stalin's Five Year Plan are spread and the anti-democrat and sponging character of it is shown. The slogans of the Ukrainian Resistance Movement call to the fight against the exploitation of the peasants and workers, for social justice, for high living standard and for independence. We give some appeals of the Ukrainian Resistance Movement:

Working People! In the fourth Five-Year Plan the Stalin spongers have made only aeroplanes, guns and tanks, but no articles which you need for your daily life! Make no preparation for war! Fight for real peace and a high living standard! Away with Stalin's imperialism!"

"Working people! Down with the inverted declarations of Stalin about the transition to Communism! We do not want to be deceived by boasting about the building of socialism. We want a free and good life! We want to fight against the Bolshevik exploitation! Down with the Stalin parasites!

"Workers! Stalin's spongers ordered the trade-Unions to organize the new socialistic Stakhanov contest! Down with the Stalin trade-unions! Down with this tool in the hands of the Stalin clique to exploit the working class! Death to the commissaries of the Stalin trade-Unions! Let the real workers be the leaders of the trade-unions! We want to fight for real democracy in the trade-unions!

"Kolkhoz farmers! The Stalin parasites enjoy their life by means of your products, while you suffer from starvation! Take the products for yourselves, for you are the producers. Take your own bread! Chase away the guards of the Kolkhoz grain! Kill the active NKVD controlling people, and their spies!

"Workers of Ukraine! The fourth Five-Year Plan is a preparation for a new war aiming at the suppression of other peoples of the world! We do not want to die for Stalin's imperialistic interests! Break all Stalin's plans wherever you can! The sooner the Stalin empire will collapse the better for you! Long live the fight of the Ukrainian people for their independent state! Long live the freedom of the peoples and the freedom of the individual!"

The leaflets of the Ukrainian Resistance Movement are brought to all parts of the Soviet Union. Recently, Moscow was plastered with the leaflets of the Ukrainian Resistance Movement. In Ukraine every pillar-box, sign-post, telegraph and milestone, railway station and railway train, buses and trams are stuck with leaflets. Often they are printed on field-presses where handmade wooden types are used. Often they have artistic engravings which tell more than the contents of the leaflets.

The contents of the propaganda of the Ukrainian Resistance Movement classifies it not only as a "subversive organization", but also as a most important political force behind the "Iron Curtain".

The Technical Service (TZ) operates the underground presses, prepares leaflets, printed materials, stores explosives, mines terrain and carries out the demolition of bridges, railway tracks, buildings and railway trains carrying supplies and war material and, at the time of the German occupation, operated the underground radio stations. It operates the famous "Insurgent V 1" which so brilliantly demolished the building of the Russian NKVD and Polish UB in the battle of Hrubieszow, on May 27 and 28, 1946. It was a joint Polish-Ukrainian underground action against the town of Hrubieszow in Poland in which the troops of VIN (Freedom and Independence), the Polish underground organization, participated along with the troops of the UPA. The action ended with the seizure of Hrubieszow. As we said above, the Ukrainian "Insurgent V 1" completely demolished the buildings where the Soviet NKVD and Polish UB troops were garrisoned, causing many casualties among them. This "Insurgent V 1" was simply Wooden Rack Launcher 28/32 cm of the German Army which could fire high explosive 280-mm rockets or incendiary 320-mm rockets. This rocket launcher and more than a hundred rockets were captured during the retreat of the German Army from Ukraine. To the duties of the Technical Service belongs also the preparation of false documents and other identification papers.

Having the territorial organization of the OUN as its chief base, the Ukrainian Insurgent Army (UPA) carries out its operations throughout Ukraine and far beyond its borders. The troops of the UPA are organized into operative groups with group commanders and their staffs at the head. The groups are divided into sectors with sector commanders and staffs at the head. The sectors are divided into detachments, the detachments into sub-detachments and the sub-detachments into squads. Each detachment has its own area of activity and the borders of its territory are crossed only in exceptional cases and on the order of the group or sector command.

The strength of UPA forces is a secret and it is impossible to give its numerical strength. Alfred Berzins, former public affairs minister of Latvia, now President of the Anti-Bolshevik Bloc of Nations (ABN), estimates it in the Washington "Times-Herald" from July 18, 1949, at 20,000 armed men, at the same time estimating the strength of the partisans operating in the Baltic states of Estonia, Latvia, Lithuania at 8,000 men. Recently, however, the number and strength of the UPA detachments was reduced to a minimum, while the strength of the territorial organization of the OUN was increased. The main stress is now laid upon the expansion of the Ukrainian Resistance Movement to the East, and upon the propaganda activities which absorb most of the personnel. Once more the character of the Ukrainian Resistance Movement changed, losing its military character, and becoming political. Nowadays it is the chief aspect of the fight of the Ukrainian Resistance Movement.

All UPA activities are planned by the Supreme Command of the UPA. Supreme Command is the main advisory body to the Supreme Commander on operations, intelligence, organization, supply, and general matters of the UPA policy. It basically consists of separate branches which cover all the proper staff and planning functions and which are groups under senior staff officers acting under supervision of a Chief of Staff.

11. The Soviet Methods of Combatting the Ukrainian Resistance Movement

In the Soviet methods of fighting the Ukrainian Resistance Movement we must distinguish two factors: (a) an ideological - political fight against the Ukrainian "nationalism" which gave birth to the Ukrainian Resistance Movement, (b) an armed terroristic fight against the Ukrainian Resistance Movement itself.

In their ideological-political fight against Ukrainian nationalism, the Bolsheviks widely use (1) misinterpretation of historic facts concerning Ukrainian history and their unscientific explanation, (2) liquidation of all free centers of Ukrainian science by means of arrests, torturings, shootings, deportation of scientific workers, (3) suppression of whole series of scholarly works that had already been published, and destruction of works which were ready for publication, (4) terrorization of the Ukrainian scientific institutes and their workers.

In consequence of such measures, science in Ukraine lost its objectivity and its value and assumed the character of a pseudo-scientific service to aid political propaganda and governmental designs.

Especially, this is true of research on Ukrainian history. As early as 1930, Prof. M.Hrushevsky, the head of the department of History at the Ukrainian Academy of Science in Kiev, and the creator of the modern historical school, was exiled. At the same time, many renowned historians, such as Slabchenko, Vasilenko, Hermaize, and Ponomarenko were liquidated. After the reoccupation of the Western Ukraine, such West-Ukrainian historians as Krypyskevych, Korduba, Terletskyj and many others were forced to make retractions, and to say that they had been led into "false nationalist paths" by Michael Hrushevsky. Ukrainian history is now to be written and taught according to Stalin's recipe of 1932, "How to write the history of the Soviet people". This new history of Ukraine has two characteristics. The first is its slanting of national affairs to the political line of the Communist government of the Soviets. The second is the adjusting of this history to Marxist dialectics; therefore it is interwoven with quotations from Marx, Engels, Lenin and Stalin. Thus, any historical work becomes ordinary Communistic literature, without any scientific value.

Because of this slant Soviet-Ukrainian historical books sharply diverge from the fundamental ideology of all Ukrainian historians outside of the Soviet-Union. Just as in the days of Tsarist Russia, the Kievan period of Ukrainian history now must be treated as a period common to both Ukrainian and Russian history, although it is a historical fact that the Russians first made their appearance as a national entity during the 12th century, in the form of the embryonic Suzdal-Rostov principality on the vast colonial stretches of the ancient Ukrainian Kievan state. Ukrainian relations with Russia are presented either one-sidedly, or completely ignored if they are inimical and impossible to explain. The treaty of Pereyasslav, 1654, concluded by Hetman Bohdan Khmelnitsky is interpreted as one of "allegiance to the Muscovite Tsar", whereas in fact Khmelnitsky concluded a treaty of alliance with Muscovy which provided that Ukraine retain full independence in all internal and external affairs. Also as during Tsarist times, Ukrainian historical personages who endeavored to free Ukraine, such as the hetmans Vyhovsky, Doroshenko and especially Mazeppa, were politically anathemized by the Reds. Hetman Ivan Mazeppa, the nationalist who declared war against Russia, is regarded as a traitor, and an enemy of the Ukrainian people. The same is said of Gen. Simon Petlura, the leader of the Ukrainian national forces in the Ukrainian War of Independence (1918-1921) and the Ukrainian struggle for independence is presented as the action of the bourgeois elements opposing the interests of the workmen and peasants of Ukraine, although exactly the contrary was the truth. The entire interpretation of Ukrainian history aims to show the paths along which Ukraine is being brought closer to Russia, under the tutelage of the Russians playing the role of the "elder brother" among the enslaved peoples, i.e. to the further enslavery of Ukraine.

After the reoccupation of the Western Ukraine the Soviets disbanded the Shevchenko Scientific Society at Lviv (which is now celebrating its seventy-fifth anniversary in emigration). For three quarters of a century, since its foundation in 1873, it has been the outstanding center of all Ukrainian scientific and scholarly work.

As to the Ukrainian language, Stalin is willing to allow its existence but he has made clear that all articles written in this language must be approved by the "big brother" of the Ukrainians, the Russian people, and by the Supreme Politbureau of the Communist Party sitting in Moscow and dictating the destinies of the entire Soviet-Union. He has made it clear that the culture of Ukraine is to be Communist-Russian culture, merely expressed in Ukrainian.

Russian Communism is trying to attack the very soul of Ukraine. It is attacking not only the leaders but also the masses. It is trying to eradicate all those principles under which the Ukrainians, like other Christian peoples, have lived for nearly one thousand years. Yet the attack too, is failing, for apart from physical extermination, the spirit of the Ukrainians is unquenchable. It can only be corrupted by the shameless rewriting of the Ukrainian past, the mutilation of the world of Ukrainian literature, and the slandering of the great men of the past and present, but truth will ultimately prevail.

The attack of the Communist Party and its agencies on Ukrainian literature grew to tremendous proportions. It began with the misinterpretation of the classics of Ukrainian literature. The fate of Shevchenko, the greatest national poet of Ukraine (1814-1861) is typical: With monotonous regularity, the Soviet critics stress his friendship with the Russian radicals of his day. They ignore his great works which emphasize cultural differences and historical diversity between Russia and Ukraine. Such works as the "Great Grave", where the poet dealt with the past of Ukraine and her relations with Russia, are entirely ommitted and the poet is only shown as a foe of the old Tsarist order and not a foe of Russian imperialism. The attack of the Russian Communists on Ukrainian literature finished with the physical extermination of Ukrainian writers and critics. A ruthless terror conducted against Ukrainian literature in 1932-1939 and after the Second World War, caused the death of hundreds of Ukrainian authors and critics. Among the hundreds of Ukrainian writers executed by the Soviets, we find talents honored and known not only in Ukraine.

After the Second World War a new wave of terror flooded the country, bringing with it new persecution of writers and artists. Despite a continual terror, it is amazing how Ukrainian literature perpetually regenerates itself. At times when all seems to be lost and extinguished, new names appear, new works are born. By the very existence of Ukrainian literature, in spite of all the cruel and ruthless persecution, the Ukrainian nation proves that it never was and never will be reconciled with the Russian occupiers. Ukrainian literature still exists and the bare fact of its existence is a miracle and proof of the unyielding spirit of the people in the struggle for independence.

At the XVIth Congress of the Ukrainian Communist Party, Prime Minister Khrushchev charged that the Ukrainian Communists failed "to organize widespread criticism of the hostile Ukrainian bourgeois Nationalist ideology in the literature and the press." He complained that "owing to this, there have been ideological mistakes and distortions, attempts to allow rebirth of the bourgeois Nationalist concepts of the historian Hrushevsky and his school, in some books, magazines, and newspapers." At the meetings of the Union of Ukrainian Writers in Kiev, several writers and editors were critized and censured for spreading theories denoting Ukrainian nationalism. They were said to have propagated "Ukrainian nationalist ideas, alien to the Soviet ideology", according to the opinion of the Politbureau. Furthermore it was charged that in their books, they had "ignored progressive leaders in Soviet literature, exaggerated the influence of Western European literature, and failed to emphasize the ties between Russian and Ukrainian literature." Several writers and poets were denounced for "forgetting fundamental ideological demands of the Party." L.Smilansky was accused because he "openly opposed the Ukrainian people and culture to the Russian people and culture". Another writer, A.Kundzich, was charged with spreading the idea of "patriarchal self-generating origins of Ukraine's people and its culture." A woman writer, V. Cherednychenko, "idealized the remote past and distorted the life of the Soviet people." L. Kovalenko, I. Pilhuk, G. Lazarevsky and Ostap Vyshnya, all critics, were severely criticized for distorting the actual conditions of Soviet life.

Premier Khrushchov's revelations, as well as all these "criticisms and self-criticisms", at the meetings of the Ukrainian writers and critics show that, despite the policy of persecution and mass deportation, the Ukrainians remain bitterly opposed to Stalin's regime and do not cease fighting for their liberation. And we must not forget that, under Soviet conditions, such "criticisms and self-criticisms" mean as usual deportation of a writer to Siberia, or in the best case expulsion from the literature.

Another subversive tool of the ideological and political fight against the Ukrainian Resistance Movement, is the slandering of it and its leaders throughout the Soviet-Union and the whole world. By this means, the Soviets aim to undermine the confidence of the Ukrainian people and of the whole world in the Ukrainian Resistance Movement. In their written and oral propaganda against the Ukrainian Resistance Movement, the Bolsheviks speak of an "independent" Ukraine as a "German" or an "Austrian" intrigue to divide "indivisible Russia". Therefore, they speak of "Ukrainian-German" Nationalists as Nazi-German "collaborators" and "traitors" who "sold Ukraine to Germans". In speaking to the Western World the Bolsheviks maintain that the Ukrainian Insurgent Army (UPA) is composed of "armed terroristic gangs which raid and pillage the villages and murder their population," or that they are "fascists", "Red Army deserters", "Vlassov army" or other "criminal elements". Even the Minister of the Ukrainian SSR Mr. D. Manuilsky, in his address delivered at the Conference of teachers of Western Ukraine on Jan. 6, 1945 (i.e. on Christmas Eve according to Greek-Catholic rite!) maintained that the UPA had "staged massacres of the Ukrainian population, committed atrocious crimes, tortures, and murders, forced the Ukrainians into German slavery, and had deceived the Ukrainian people by saying that they had gone underground to struggle against the Germans".

The spreading of lies about the Ukrainian Resistance Movement is widely used in Bolshevik propaganda. Now the UPA and the Ukrainian Resistance Movement are no longer called the "hirelings of German Nazi fascists" but the "spies" and "diversionists" either of Vatican or of "American warmongers". The term "Ukrainian-German" Nationalists has disappeared from the Soviet press and, gradually, has changed to "Ukrainian-American" Nationalists. The Soviets are willing for the people to believe that the UPA has entered the "service of American fascists". In January 1948, at the celebration of the "30th Anniversary" of their bloody and barbarous conquest of Ukraine, Premier Khrushchov delivered a lengthy harangue against the Ukrainian Resistance Movement, and, of course, against the United States and Great Britain in the presence of Molotov himself who was dispatched by the Kremlin to deliver "a message of friendship" to the Ukrainian people from Stalin. Khrushchov claimed that the USA and Great Britain are actively supporting the Ukrainian underground. After admitting that the Ukrainian Resistance Movement had been giving some serious trouble to the MVD-MGB and the entire Soviet administration in

Ukraine, Khrushchev called upon the Ukrainians themselves to "exterminate" the Ukrainian nationalist elements, "lackeys of the Anglo-Saxon powers, the worst enemies of democracy and humanity."

The last appellation - "lackeys of the Anglo-Saxon powers" - is significant because of the time as well as the linking of the USA and Great Britain with Ukrainian underground. First, it becomes evident that the opposition against the totalitarian power of Soviet Russia in Ukraine is not negligible; second, the Russians apparently intend to identify the Ukrainian Resistance Movement with the United States and Great Britain, now the No 1 enemies in the Russian hate-campaign against the West.

But this is not the first time that the Russians have found it expedient to tag the Ukrainian Liberation Movement as a foreign intrigue, dumped upon Ukrainian soil. For example, at the time of the Polish uprising, 1863/64, the Ukrainian movement was branded as a "Polish intrigue". Before the First World War it was called as "German intrigue", after the fall of the Ukrainian democratic state in 1921 all Ukrainian patriots were branded "agents of capitalist intervention" and were dealt with accordingly. In the early thirties when fascism and nazism appeared on the horizon, all Ukrainians wishing liberation from Russia became "Hitler's and Mussolini's spies." Significantly, this calumny was skilfully disseminated by Russian agents in the countries of the West, especially the United States. As a result, even today, when one country after another falls under Soviet despotism, there still are Americans and sundry "experts" who cling to this pro-Soviet line.

It is extremely disturbing to note the degree to which the Russians have succeeded with their propaganda. Ukrainian insurgents, these simple people, akin to American Revolutionary heroes, have been accepted as "bandits", "fascist hirelings", "SS-men", etc. by certain organs of the American democratic press. In this case the American pressmen have swallowed not only the Red bait hook, but also the line and sinker.

The truth is one and it is "indivisible". The truth is the Ukrainians are now fighting for those ideals which are common to the whole Western civilized world and it is the chief reason for such a hate propaganda against them by the Soviet "super-democrats" of Moscow.

It must be emphasized here that the lies spread by the Bolshiviks are very easily accepted by the Western world. The basis of the ideal of a free press has been the idea that by informing the people of the true facts involved, they will sooner and better draw true and logical conclusions, and their resultant acts will thereby be just and of benefit to the common welfare. This idealistic policy is daily implemented by the American and Western European press in their coverage of what goes on in American or Western European life. But in regard to events which take place in eastern Europe, the exceptions from this golden rule are very frequent. Unfortunately not only the Ukrainian Resistance Movement is misrepresented and maligned all over the world, but also the story of the heroic Ukrainian Resistance against both the Nazis and the Communists during the last war, and the facts of national and religious persecutions by the Soviets, today, are completely ignored or distorted, if not silenced by the world press under the influence of Kremlin propagandists and their press agents all over the world.

Experience in Ukraine with Soviet tyranny tells us that the Soviets often use deceit and lies to further their political ambitions. Lenin himself stated that "we have to use any ruse, dodges, tricks, cunning, unlawful methods, concealment, veiling of truth" in daily political manipulation. By this weapon of Bolshevik strategy, the Ukrainians and their sympathetic friends everywhere were denounced as "fascists" by the genuine scarlet fascists in Moscow. By means of this weapon, any group in the world courageous enough to raise its voice against the savageries of Soviet dictatorship is conveniently dubbed "fascist" by the Soviet political opium dealers. By means of this weapon, any patriot-fighter for liberation of a nation subjugated by Reds is dubbed "bandit", any democrat - "bourgeois nationalist", anyone who criticizes Soviet system - a "warmonger". The ideological basis of this Soviet weapon is a Muscovite megalomania based on a bottomless immorality, sanctioning as morally good every lie, falsehood, or crime against a non-Communist person, nation or state.

The old world of Western civilization must defend itself against the Soviet lying propaganda, or surrender to Communist totalitarianism. The Ukrainian Resistance Movement can be its valuable ally in the fight, not only against the complete enslavement of the body, of the free minds and the free souls of the rest of the world.

In their armed-terroristic fight against the Ukrainian Resistance Movement and its armed branche, the UPA, the Bolsheviks applied the following measures: (a) broad actions carried out by the army and police troops supported by artillery, tanks, and air-planes against the UPA units, (b) the garrisoning and the prolonged blockading of villages and woods in the insurgent territories, (c) the sudden round-ups in villages and woods, (d) the deforestation of the country by burning the forests, (e) the use of bacteriological warfare, (f) the organization of planned starvation of the Ukrainian population, (g) the public torturing and murdering of the Ukrainian insurgents, and their relatives as well as murdering of the Ukrainian population, (h) the organization of a spy-system and of a network of agents-provocateurs, (i) organization of special gangs for fighting the UPA, (j) the forcible deportation of the population to Siberian and Kazakhstan deserts and farther east and north, (k) the economic pillaging of the population, (l) the amnesty and propaganda campaign against the Ukrainian Resistance Movement.

During the spring and summer of 1944, the Red Army began advancing into insurgent territory. The Soviet commanders decided that they were sufficiently strong to deliver one sweeping coup de grace to the Ukrainian Insurgent Army (UPA). Consequently, the Red commanders worked out an almost brilliant plan for combatting the UPA-North operating in Volhynia and Polessia. They aimed to divide it into two parts separating it at the same time from the UPA West and South. The Soviets decided to start their first action against the UPA-North in April, 1944, just after the seizing of the territory from the Germans. The Red Command thought that if one expedition force could pin the UPA forces in the Polessia marshes, and the other sweep around their left flank in the Kovel area, the chief mobile force consisting of 30,000 elite troops, largely cavalry and tanks, would encircle the main UPA forces of the UPA-North in the Kremyanets area and capture or destroy them. The plan was carried out.

The proceedings during such an action which became a model for all future actions, against the UPA are as follows. First the insurgent territory is saturated with spies weeks in advance. Then the troops are concentrated in the villages and woods in the vicinity of the target. Strong reconnaissance troops are sent to find out the position of the enemy. The heavy equipment is moved up and the attack is opened. The woods and villages are advanced upon by the troops in skirmish line. The insurgent nests are attacked and the insurgents are pushed back into the waiting arms of the blocking forces called "bags".

The first action against the UPA-North began in April, 1944, by blocking the Kovel area in Western Volhynia. Here 2 Red army divisions were used in combatting the UPA and in cutting it off from the front rear area. Another expedition force started blocking the access to the Polessia marshes in the north. Here another 2 divisions were used. The chief mobile force consisting of 3 divisions supported by air-force and 2 tank brigades encircled the Kremyanets area in southern Volhynia in April, 1944 and aimed at the destruction of the main forces of the UPA-North having their base in this area. The action ended with a big battle at Hurby, on April 24, 1944. This battle ended with a partial victory for the Ukrainian insurgents of whom 5,000 UPA fighters were able to escape from the encirclement causing the attacking Soviets heavy casualties (at least 33% of the total strength of the Red infantry). However, the Ukrainian casualties were also very high. Many Ukrainians were either killed or wounded and Gen. A. Stupnytsky, chief of staff of the UPA fell in this battle.

The Ukrainian Insurgent Army (UPA) survived many actions of this kind. The first action against the UPA base in the Carpathians, the "Black forest" (prov. Stanislav) was carried out along the same scheme by 2 Red divisions between 1st and 4th of November, 1944. This attack was forced back by forces of the "Black Forest" causing the Soviets heavy casualties. Immediately all rayon centers in the vicinity of the "Black Forest" were attacked by the advancing victorious insurgent units. Unsuccessful also was the attack of 1 Red Army division and of numerous police troops against the so-called "Hutsul Republic" in the "Black Mountains" (south-eastern part of the Carpathians). This started the Khrushchev-Ryassny offensive of April, 1945. Concerning this operation, the commander of the UPA group, "Hoverla", stated in his report of June 30, 1945: "The battalions of my group pushed back the attack of the 271st Red Rifle Division supported by many NKVD troops, and raided 8 administrative centers. The death roll of the enemy in these incidents was 3,975 persons including 6 majors, 10 captains, 30 lieutenants, 17 NKVD officers and party leaders and 1,385 persons wounded. 21 track-loads and 5 locomotives were destroyed, 9 bridges were blown up and 22 machine guns, 103 sub-machine guns, 29 automatic rifles, 321 rifles, 38 pistols and ammunition were captured. Our losses: 215 killed and 129 wounded fighters. 20 fighters tore themselves to pieces by using handgrenades in order not to be captured alive by the enemy."

Still other actions of such kind were: (1) the attack on the forest block Yaniv-Zovkva-Yavoriv to the north of Lviv, in June, 1945, carried out by 2 divisions supported by tanks and airplanes, (2) the simultaneous attack of 2 divisions on the forest Lopatyn-Hrycevola-Toporiv-Triyca north-east of Lviv in June and July of 1945, (3) the second operation against the "Black Forest" in July, 1945, carried out by 3 Red divisions with the support of the air-force and NKVD-troops, (4) the operation against the Zavadivsky forest between Kovel and Volodymyr Volynsky in July, 1945. All these operations aimed at the total destruction of the Ukrainian Insurgent Army (UPA) and were part of the scheme of the big Khrushchev-Ryassny offensive in 1945 in which 3 army corps and many divisions of NKVD troops were used against the UPA in the provinces, Stanislav, Drohobych, Lviv, and Volhynia (Lutsk). This offensive had to be withdrawn because the Red Army units used in it showed themselves to be rather unreliable in the fight against the UPA.

The big Ryassny-Moskalenko offensive against the UPA started in December, 1945, and lasted until June, 1946. It was preceded by the attack against the UPA mountain nests of Hoverla and Chornohora, in October and November, 1945. This time 3 elite NKVD divisions could not succeed in ejecting the Ukrainian insurgents from the Carpathian mountains. The NKVD-ites used an unheard of terror against the mountaineers (Hutsuls) and tried to annihilate the population of mountainous rayons by a terrible blockade which caused hunger and typhus among the civilian population. The UPA carried out a general inoculation against typhus and shipped large quantities of food from Rumania and Hungary into the rayons threatened by starvation.

The Ryassny-Moskalenko offensive against the UPA practically ended with the assassination of Gen.Col.Moskalenko. Even this offensive could not prevent the Ukrainian population from boycotting the February, 1946, elections to the Supreme Soviet, and could not succeed in liquidating the Ukrainian Resistance Movement.

The last big action of this kind was the Swierszczewski offensive against the UPA-West from February to July, 1947. Gen. Swierszczewski was killed during this offensive on March 27, 1947. Following his assassination, a tripartite pact among Soviet-Russia, Poland, and Czechoslovakia was concluded aiming at the total destruction of the UPA-West. Large enemy forces were thrown into action. According to this anti-Partisan pact, Poland brought into action 1 motorized infantry corps of three divisions, the Soviet Command of the Sub-Carpathian Military Area at Lvov brought 1 tank division and special anti-partisan units, and Czechoslovakia brought 1 mountain brigade. All these troops were supported by the Soviet and Polish air-force. Fierce fighting continued in a large area during the spring and summer of 1947. The center of this anti-partisan action was the district Lisko in south-eastern Poland. A Soviet tank brigade passed the Soviet-Polish frontier and advanced against the main insurgent force. With the help of Polish troops, it tried to encircle the insurgents, but the latter succeeded in escaping southwards and reached Slovakia and Carpatho-Ukraine. Another group of Ukrainian insurgents passed the river San and reached Ukrainian territory hiding itself in the forests north of Lviv. Still another group of the UPA escaped northwards in the direction of the Polessia marshes. The insurgent group under the command of Mjr. Bayda crossed into Slovakia and reached the US Zone of occupation in Germany in September, 1947, after a march of 1500 km across Czechoslovakia and Austria.

At the time of these big operations the Bolshevists did not cease systematically harrassing the UPA by blockading the villages and woods in the insurgent territory, as well as by raiding the villages and woods. They tried to interfere with UPA preparations for winter quarters, winter stores, clothing and other shops. The garrisoning of soldiers in the insurgent territory lasted for the duration of the Ryassny-Moskalenko offensive in 1946. This assignment the Soviets gave to the special NKVD-NKGB troops with full power of murdering any Ukrainian they pleased. They were allowed to rape the women and to pillage the houses. The Ukrainian Resistance Movement could write a big "Black Book" about such despicable maltreatment, atrocious crimes, tortures and murders committed by these gangs of NKVD - a book no less terrifying than the accusations drawn up by the peoples of Europe against the German Nazis. They ravaged like ferocious beasts, and tortured the population in order to intimidate the Ukrainian people. The terror was unparalleled even in the history of Muscovy which knows the "Oprichina" of Ivan the Terrible and the "okhranka" of the Tsars. But they did not succeed in breaking down the spirit of the Ukrainian people. They only caused an unlimited hatred of the Soviet regime and nothing more.

During the big Ryassny-Moskalenko offensive against the UPA, the Bolsheviks used large scale deforestation of the country as the means of fight against the UPA concentrations. As usual the forests were burned down. The deforestation was usually limited to the area actually known to be held by partisans. The determined object was encircled by the NKVD troops and the encircling lines had to prevent the insurgents from escaping from the burning forest. On a given signal air-planes threw incendiary bombs on the forest and inflamed it in different places. If the insurgents were in object, they had either to be burned alive, or to break out. There were many actions of this kind in the Western Ukraine. By Spring, 1946, all pine woods in the Kovel area (Volhynia) were completely burned down. By Summer, 1946, this action embraced the area of the "Black Forest" and the "Hrycevola-Lopatyn" Forest in the province of Lviv. The material losses caused by such a "deforestation" were tremendous. Only between Toporiv and Triyca in the north-eastern part of the province of Lviv, nearly 5,000 ha of forest were completely burned down.

Despite the fact that bacteriological warfare is interdicted by international treaties, the Bolsheviks used it in the fight against the UPA. The Ukrainian Resistance Movement has many records in its archives that such means were used both against the UPA and against the Ukrainian civilian population. The Bolsheviks knew that the UPA was buying antitoxin on the black market, so, in 1946, the Soviet agents began to sell poisoned injections in large quantities. The victims of these injections died in tortures. Soon the trick was discovered and the UPA ceased buying medicines in the local black market and began buying them in Poland, Czechoslovakia, and even in Germany. The UPA had to overcome great difficulties in mastering this situation. It organized whole expeditions to buy medicines in Warsaw, Cracow, Katowice, Budapest and Bratislava, Vienna and Prague and to bring them back to its bases in the Carpathians. This is another story of the fanatic heroism of Ukrainian men and women in their fight against the vile and contemptibly low methods of the "great eastern Super-Democracy".

We have already mentioned the planned starvation of the mountain population in the Carpathians. By applying a terrible blockade of the mountain rayons, the Soviets aimed to deprive the UPA of its natural bases. The same method was applied in the marshy rayons of Polessia, which had been another natural base of the UPA. In this area the Ukrainian people were not allowed to move from village to village and no food was brought into the cooperatives. Intensive fishing in the Prypjat river and in its tributaries ordered by the UPA was the sole possible means of rescue. The population of the Carpathians was saved by the large quantities of food brought in by armed UPA expeditions from Hungary and Rumania. Under the protection of armed detachments of the UPA, the Ukrainian mountaineers from the threatened rayons, went to Hungary and Rumania and brought back necessary quantities of food to replenish the stores in the last weeks before the new harvest.

Alarming news coming from Carpatho-Ukraine confirms the rumors that large scale hunger and starvation broke out in 1948. Famine raged in such traditionally rich and fertile areas as the districts Uzhorod, Mukachiv and Berehovo. The probable reason is that the Soviets confiscated the bulk of the crop in order to force Ukrainian peasants into the much hated collective farms.

The Soviet sponsored famine is not a new instrument for them in attaining their economical and political ends. It is recalled that in the years 1932-1933 millions of Ukrainian peasants died from starvation. Apparently Moscow is now using the same device again in Western Ukraine and in Carpatho-Ukraine, which not only succeeds in introducing collectivization, but in exterminating the recalcitrant Ukrainian as well.

It is impossible to speak without a feeling of boundless anger and indignation at the savageries committed by the Ryassny-Moskalenko troops during their big offensive against the UPA, and the peaceful Ukrainian population. All these methods are the living mockery of "Freedom from Fear". "The function of compulsion inside the country has ceased, has withered away," Stalin announced in 1939. "The exploiters are no more and there is no one to suppress any more." Why if "there is no one to suppress any more" was it necessary to apply such sadistic methods for the extermination of the Ukrainian people, in 1946? Why was it necessary to cut off heads with axes, to saw the bodies of captured insurgents in two, to strangle them with ropes and to burn them in locked houses, to bury them alive and to slaughter whole families including small children? Why was it necessary to execute all this torturing in public? In the village squares of the Western Ukraine captured insurgents were boiled and roasted alive, the girls were violated in public, the wounded were summarily executed and the whole population of the "insurgent villages" were slaughtered systematically until but a few were left in the ruins of their villages. All of this, in order to "edify" the citizens and to compel them to obey the Bolshevik criminals.

The atrocities which were committed in the name of the "people" were not accidental abuses by the Ryassny-Moskalenko special troops. The "Red Terror" was a recognized and integral element in the process of subjugating the nation to the Bolshevik will. Lenin himself declared "No dictatorship of the Proletariat is to be thought of without terror and violence." And this terror and violence was applied en masse in the Western Ukraine during the sorrowful days of Spring and Summer, 1946. Even the corpses and graves of the dead insurgents were dishonored by the Bolshevik beast in uniform.

500 years ago, Ivan the Terrible, Tsar from 1544 to 1584 introduced into Russian life the peculiar institution which has continued to exist until the present day: the Secret Political Police. Ivan called the directing organ of this police, the Oprichina and its members the Oprichniki. Their duty was to ferret out disloyalty to the Tsar and to punish it with the most severe cruelty. Ivan the Terrible's Oprichina had become the Prikaz of the Peter the "Great" and the Okhrana of the Tsars, then Lenin's Cheka, then Stalin's GPU, then his NKVD, MVD and MGB. Its name had changed, but its task remained unchanged: to smell out and sweep away ruthlessly all opposition to the dictator. Its ear was everywhere. NKVD-MGB-MVD developed spying to a fine art and made it the dominant motive in Russian life. In every establishment, school, institution there is a "spetsotdiel", a branch of the MVD-MGB which openly spies on every worker, every pupil, every employee. Beside the "special department" there are hundreds of thousands of "secsots" (secret spies) bought with money, or forced by fear. Every second Russian might be a spy.

In the first days after their arrival into the Western Ukraine the Bolsheviks tried to organize a network of "secsots" among the Ukrainian population. For this purpose, they arrested the Ukrainian youth en masse and afterwards turned them loose. This complicated the task of the UPA because it was known that among these boys and girls hundreds were pressed into the services of the NKVD. The UPA and SB had to check all persons set free to find out whether they were "secsots" or not. This required much checking work on the part of the UPA and SB, but they preferred to do that than to "liquidate" all suspects as was intended by the NKVD.

Having had no success in building up a "secsot" network among the Ukrainian population, the Bolsheviks lay special stress on placing their agents in the UPA and OUN attempting to disorganize them from the inside. Thus, initially, they set free all prisoners taken in battles in order to mislead the counter-agents of the UPA and SB. Of course, it was a hard task to determine who had volunteered for the job of an agent-provocateur and who had not. The recruited agents-provocateurs tried to infiltrate the ranks of the UPA and to report on proceedings. To dispel any possible doubts the NKVD created situations which would clear their agents from any suspicion. It organized "break-outs" from prisons, "flight" from detention camps, etc. But the UPA, and SB knew that the odds were great against such a freed prisoner being a stooge. Therefore, all those who returned had to pass through a careful screening and observation, before they were again admitted into services or were doomed. Having once been in Bolshevik hands creates the highest suspicion. Such an agent-provocateur can sit in the underground bunker for months doing nothing suspicious and trying to appear O.K. The Bolsheviks do not rush such agents into action knowing that the more their man has got into the UPA confidence the more he can achieve.

A certain number of the Ukrainian insurgents, softened up by the Soviet amnesty, went out of the woods and took up residence in the Bolshevik controlled areas. To encourage this group the Bolsheviks let the first groups go free. Some of them were afterwards selected for provocation jobs. They were used in the assassination of underground leaders, and to disclose the underground shelters and stores. The Bolsheviks expected the Ukrainian SB to act discriminately and to kill the amnestid fighters thus creating a tension among the population. But SB proceeded cautiously and acted promptly in checked cases. Victims who agreed to cooperate with NKVD were between two fires and sometimes committed suicide or tried to hide themselves.

Another method was to send "rats" to the UPA. Red army and police officers with an excellent knowledge of the Ukrainian language or sometimes without if they were Georgians, Uzbeks, or the like, went to the UPA, presented themselves as anti-Bolsheviks and offered their services. They tried to get into the confidence of the UPA and did not refuse any means to achieve it. A Georgian, a major of NKVD and an agent-provocateur on a big scale, was admitted for service in the UPA. Trying to get the full confidence of the command he discovered the network of minor Bolshevik agents within the ranks of the UPA, put them before the UPA court-martial and executed the death sentence, hanging them with his own hands after the trial. Of course, he was allowed to do that by the all-powerful NKVD in order to get, in this way, a higher position in the ranks of the UPA and the full confidence of the UPA. In 1947, NKVD Cpt. Chereschukin ordered an agent-provocateur to kill NKVD Major Nosov, the chief of MGB in the rayon administration and former Red partisan, in order to get the full confidence of the dangerous insurgent group in this rayon which had not been willing to admit the agent-provocateur into its ranks. The shocking story of this assassination was told in the UPA leaflets under the heading: "Why was Comrade Nosov killed?" and now retold by the Ukrainian newspaper "Ukrainian Tribune" in its coverage from June 30,1949. Another fact illustrating the Bolshevik methods in setting their agents-provocateurs within the ranks of the UPA was told in the reports of the Ukrainian Resistance Movement. One day, in 1946, a "political prisoner" was brought into a village office near Lviv. He was under the guard of 2 NKVD officers and 4 NKVD men. The population of this village was called into the office and asked to "recognize" the man. Nobody knew him. Asked about his name the "prisoner" did not answer the questions at all and was severely beaten accordingly. During the questioning, one of the NKVD officers put his pistol on the table. Suddenly the "prisoner" seized the pistol from the table, shot down another officer of NKVD who was in his way and ran from the room. The ordered "chase" brought no results. The "prisoner" could not be found because the local population gave him protection. He told the man who gave him shelter that he was an officer of the UPA and asked him to contact the next group of the UPA. It was done. But there, despite this performance of shooting down the NKVD officer he was taken on suspicion and was soon disclosed as an officer of the NKVD sent to the UPA with a special job. The whole "theater" of the shooting in a village-office was organized by NKVD in order to gain the confidence of the local population and the "dead" officer was a political prisoner dressed up as an officer of the NKVD.

The main efforts of the NKVD in combatting the Ukrainian Resistance Movement are based on setting a network of the agents-provocateurs within the ranks of the UPA and of affiliated organizations. But many of these efforts, according to the secret instructions of Gen.Saburov, chief of MGB in the province of Drohobych, failed because of excellent counter-measures by the Ukrainian SB.

In combatting the Ukrainian Resistance Movement, the Bolsheviks often use false bands of allegedly Ukrainian insurgents. The Bolsheviks dressed as Ukrainian insurgents, invade the Ukrainian villages and pillage them in order to evoke the opposition of the population to the Ukrainian Resistance Movement. In other cases such "insurgents" ask for shelter and help in order to find out what people sympathize with the UPA. In the beginning of the struggle against the Soviets, such a masquerade was very dangerous and caused much harm, as the Ukrainian population showed an open sympathy to every manifestation of the Ukrainian Resistance Movement. At present such methods are very well known all over Ukraine and, therefore, cannot have any success. The alleged "insurgents" who come to the village without contacts with the local representatives of the Ukrainian Resistance Movement, receive no aid and support from the Ukrainian population.

The bands recruited from former insurgents and from the worst characters called "istrebiteli" are also very dangerous. They know the local conditions and the language very well. Extreme effort had to be used to neutralize them. They were exterminated and are being exterminated without pity. Now, their ranks are considerably thinned and they limit their activity to guarding warehouses and administrative buildings.

In order to combat the Ukrainian Resistance Movement the Soviets ordered the registration of the Ukrainian population. All inhabitants had to be registered in the local soviet office and the lists of the present population had to be stuck on the door. By February, 1946, the Bolsheviks began to confiscate the property of the Ukrainians whose relatives were with the UPA. When a shot was fired in the village, the Soviets used to burn down the section of the houses from which the shot came and to murder on the spot the people of the neighboring houses. In the village of Berlohy, county Kalusz, the Bolsheviks murdered 53 innocent peasants as a reprisal for the murdering of 1 Bolshevik. Many incidents of public torturing, murdering and pillaging the Ukrainians were reported from all parts of Ukraine.

Soon the Bolsheviks realized that the only means of exterminating the Ukrainian Resistance Movement was to deport the Ukrainian people who give their full support to the Ukrainian Resistance Movement. As early as 1945, the Bolsheviks started their famous deportations to Siberia and Kazakhstan. The Bolsheviks then picked out some UPA sympathizers in order to intimidate the remaining population. In 1946, they started the mass deportation, which continues even now. In the night of October 20-21, 1947, the Bolsheviks staged an unprecedented deportation which aimed to deport 500,000 to 800,000 people, or one fifth to one fourth of the population of the Western Ukraine.

A month before the action, the MVD collected barred cattle cars at all the railroad stations. Units of the MVD-MGB forces, "istrebiteli" (destruction battalions) and units of the Soviet army were billeted all over the countryside under the pretext of operations against the resistance groups.

The majority of the locally prominent people were entered on the deportation lists on charges of contact with the Ukrainian Resistance Movement, of having relatives abroad, of having "collaborated" with the Germans, etc.

After the preparations, the villages were surrounded and the deportees arrested. The whole action took twenty-four hours. The deportees were allowed to take with them only luggage they were able to carry, and no information was vouchsafed on their destination. Later it transpired that the majority was taken to Kazakhstan.

Those who managed to weather the fatal twenty-four hours in hiding, have not been troubled since, and are probably safe until the next deportation.

Great new deportations have taken place in March and April, 1949 from the southern part of former East Galicia and the Kiev province. In many parts of Ukraine the population are in a state of panic for fear of deportation. Often the MVD drags the people directly from their places of work to the deportation trains. The general spirit is one of revolt and partisan activities have sprung up with new force, especially in the Eastern Carpathians and Volhynia. The Soviet authorities combat the Ukrainian Resistance Movement by deporting the inhabitants of whole villages as soon as any of them are suspected of helping the partisans.

That the present deportation is a really large scale action is substantiated by the fact that two regular divisions of the Soviet army have been transferred to Ukraine to help the MVD in the great round-ups. These two divisions have come from Turkestan.

Foreseeing the deportation, the Ukrainian Resistance Movement issued printed instructions how to behave in case of deportation. They ordered the Ukrainian population to organize an active and passive resistance against the deportation, to hide themselves in the woods and forests, to erect special underground shelters and hiding places in order to avoid deportation. Of course, the UPA detachments stood in defense of the deportees with all their forces. Here we give a report of a person who escaped the present deportation: "In the spring of 1948 the Bolsheviks began a forcible collectivization in the districts of Zhovkva and Rava. Many peasants were arrested, among them the escapee. He was accused of campaigning against collectivization. All arrested were transferred to the infamous "Brygidki prison in Lviv, where at least 400 other Ukrainians were detained. Most of them were peasant youths, including children between the years 10 and 14, who were arresting for putting wreaths on the graves of UPA soldiers killed in action. On June 24, 1948, all the arrested were taken from the "Brigidki" prison and put on a cattle train destined for the interior parts of the Soviet Union. The transport had 50 cars, each containing 50 men. Leaving Lviv at night, the train was stopped a few kilometres outside the city by a raiding party. The cars were broken open and their occupants freed. One of the attackers identified the raiding party as the UPA and advised the released Ukrainian youths to hide from the Bolsheviks for "very soon we will need all able-bodied men for an important task." The MVD guards were either killed or taken away by the insurgents." (Ukrainian Word, a newspaper of the Ukrainians in the British zone, from Dec. 5, 1948)

The population obeyed the orders of the Ukrainian Resistance Movement and, thus, the Bolsheviks could deport only 150,000 men and women instead of 500,000. The rest remained in the country. Settlers from Russia who were resettled on the farms of the deportees were summoned to leave for their homes, and, in case of resistance, they were forcibly evicted. Only Ukrainians from other provinces were allowed to settle on the farms of the deportees.

The amnesty and propaganda campaign was an endeavor of the Communist Party and the Soviet government of Ukraine to break down the morale of the Ukrainian Resistance Movement. To strengthen their appeals, the Soviets carried out blockades of the insurgent territory by massed troops, and then tried to whitewash themselves by blaming the underground for hardships on the population caused by their counter-measures against the UPA. They also forced the innocent people to sign the surrender application and, afterwards they boasted of the great number of illegal partisans who allegedly gave up.

Before July, 1945, there were three appeals to the Ukrainian insurgents issued with great publicity: September 1944, December 1944, and May 1945. In the last appeal, the Soviets boasted of their victory over Germany and threatened that this was the last appeal and that it would be followed by a merciless destruction of the Ukrainian Resistance Movement. In January, 1945, the Minister for Foreign Affairs of the Ukrainian SSR, D.Manuilsky, delivered a great speech before the teachers' convention in Lviv. While his harangue was entirely devoted to the Ukrainian Resistance Movement he promised in the name of the Soviet government to "pardon" all who would cease their anti-Soviet activities. Anti-Soviet activities, however, increased considerably after this speech and elections to the Supreme Soviet were boycotted everywhere in the Western Ukraine.

One of the last "mermaid's songs" was sung by the "Ukrainian" Minister of NKVD Gen.V.Ryassny on Nov.15, 1945, and was quoted above. It was distributed in the country by the spring and summer of 1946. There were not many that obeyed this order. Often the surrendering came from "holers", i.e. unorganized partisans and Red army deserters who carried on a warfare of their own. The insurgents organized in the UPA seldom participated in such amnesty schemes. One of their rules is that no one shall be captured alive and this rule is consistently observed by the boys and girls of the UPA.

Following the well-tested methods of the Russian MVD, the Czech Minister of the Interior issued an appeal to the "members of the UPA in Czechoslovakia. In it, the Czech Communist appealed to the Ukrainians as follows: "Kill your commanders, throw away your weapons and report to the NB'(the Czech Security Police). It concluded: "Surrender! You will live and work! The Slav truth will win!"

There is no doubt that the fight against the Bolsheviks is very hard and difficult. But the Ukrainian Resistance Movement is waging an implacable war against the Soviet forces. It is very efficient in fighting Soviet forces despite the fact that the occupation army and police forces have heavy weapons while the Ukrainian Resistance Movement has none, and that everything must be seized, including munitions, because the Ukrainian fighters are not supplied and encouraged by the West. And if the might of Soviet Russia has not conquered them yet, it will n e v e r conquer them!

12. The Ukrainian Resistance Movement and the Western Powers

The United States has repeatedly shown its sympathy with the rights of peoples large and small to their self-determination. As early as January 8, 1918, President Wilson laid down "Fourteen Points" and proclaimed the right of self-determination for all peoples. Not only that, but as early as August, 1941, President Roosevelt and Prime-Minister Churchill made a significant Pronouncement, known as the Atlantic Charter, the principles of which bear upon the rights of people to select governments of their own choice by the will of the people themselves. The declaration of President Truman (Truman Doctrine) to the American Congress is in keeping with the above mentioned acts which represent the finest ideals of the American spirit.

Unfortunately, thanks to forces in the United States which still stand for the "indivisibility" of "holy" (and despotic) "Mother Russia", attempts are being made to divert the United States from playing the role of the defender of all enslaved peoples of Eastern Europe. These forces, it seems make the United States forget its international pledges, as expressed in the Atlantic Charter, the Four Freedoms, and the Truman Doctrine. To our amazement and regret, American public opinion, and to some extent official policy, are to this day influenced greatly by these forces in the government, universities and the press.

The question arises: What will the United States do in the event of a showdown with Russia? Will a policy of errors continue to govern the American over-all pattern for Eastern Europe, or will a realistic policy be evolved - a policy which will fully incorporate the factor of the anti-Soviet struggle of the enslaved nations? A positive program, aiming at the total dismemberment of the Russian Empire and the substitution of a series of sovereign and independent states, would be the only unfailing stimulus for the non-Russian peoples to fight Stalin. Such a program would ensure success in the event of war. It would be disastrous, for example to import Kerensky and Co., or another Vlassov man who would not only maintain the Russian Empire, but try to expand is as well. For the Ukrainians, Belorussians, Cossacks, Armenians, Azerbaidjans, Georgians, Turkestanians and the people of the three Baltic states, the only change would be a turning back of history's clock a century to the autocracy of the Tsars.

The national question of the Soviet-Union, the foremost problem of today's politics, has been too much neglected by the Anglosaxon world. The Communists and their fellow-travellers are spreading abroad the cry about "ethnic democracy" in the Soviets, about the first example in the world of the solution of the national problems in a country which is a mixture of nationalities. The existence in the Soviets of an "ethnic democracy", to use the phrase of Wallace, is just as much a bluff as is the existence of liberty, democracy, a free press, economic equality, etc. in that land of totalitarian dictatorship and terror. Ethnic democracy has never existed in the Soviets as it never existed in Russia. And it does not exist there today as it will not exist in any Russia, be it "white", or "red", "fascist" or "democratic".

What of the future? A hungry and agonizing world stands helpless, unable to make peace and return to prosperity and order, and in fear of a new war inevitably to come. Communist intrigues, fifth columns, and partisan bands are roaming to extend still further the domain where human liberties are no more and where concentration camps and religious persecution are the order of the day. The United Nations in its present form seems to have only the choice of relapsing into futility or submitting to the masters of the Kremlin. A monopoly of atomic weapons is a very illusive one. The probability of the possession of the atomic bomb by the USSR constitutes an unimaginable danger to the Western nations and to world peace. There is no time to waste. The Soviet-Union prepares aggression against the Western nations. Its established and active network of fifth columns throughout the world, its past record of broken promises and treaties, its present record of obstruction in the making of a constructive policy with the Western nations, as well as its purposeful neglect of reciprocal relations with the West prove conclusively the immense danger the aggressive Soviet power is to the Western civilization.

It is becoming increasingly evident in the United States that many objective minds studying the problem of Eastern Europe are ridding themselves of the myth of the homo-geneity of Russia; an idea which is till propagated by numerous Russian emigrants. The unspeakable disservice done by these writers to the interests of the United States and of the democratic principle in the East, might well result in a repetition of the fatal mistake made by the democratic world at the end of World War I. when the Western democratic powers supported all the anti-democratic, non-communist Russian forces to the fatal detriment of the one solely genuine democratic force, that of Ukrainian liberation. The inevitable outcome was, as we know, the perpetuation of the Russian Empire as a "red" regime instead of "white".

Therefore, the artificial political structure of the Russian Empire, now in the form of the USSR, must be decisively eliminated. The Russian Empire must be dismembered and replaced by a political reconstruction of Eastern Europe along lines of ethnographic validity, with the institution of the right of self-determination of peoples and of democratic processes of government. It must at last be recognized that the political system resulting from Russian military dominance in Eastern Europe has always been and continues to be founded upon force, fraud and fear.

As soon as the dangerous myths that becloud an objective understanding of the situation in the Soviet-Union are dispelled the way will become clear for consideration of a policy aiming at the reconstruction of Eastern Europe. It requires little imagination to perceive the fundamental fact that Soviet ambitions for world conquest rest upon the basic solidity of the Soviet Eurasia of which Ukraine is an indispensable segment. The separation of Ukraine from the Soviet Eurasia would be one of the greatest blows possible to Russian ambitions for the conquest of world. Without Ukraine, and the other non-Russian entities, the Russian colossus would be deprived of the essential requisites for its expansion projects. The critical importance of Ukraine, especially, cannot, therefore, be neglected in the foreign and military policies of the United States.

It is not only the numerical strength of the Ukrainian nation that would be of importance. General Eisenhower in his address to newspapermen before taking over the presidency of Columbia university, gave his opinion of the war potential of the Soviet Union. Asked by one of the correspondents, which part of Europe and Asia has the most strategical importance for the security of the United States, he declared without hesitation: "Europe west of the Volga is the most important part from our viewpoint."

The most important part of Europe west of the Volga River is Ukraine. Although Gen. Eisenhower, for reasons of his own, did not name it, geopolitically, the Soviet power is concentrated in Ukraine and radiates from it into the Baltic and Northern Europe, into the Danubian Valley and the Mediterranean, into the Persian Gulf and the Near East, either southward to Iraq (Mesopotamia) or south-westward through Turkey, Syria, Palestine, and across the Suez into Egypt. Thus Ukraine constitutes a wide assembling place which could be used either by Stalin as the starting point for military conquest, or by the Western nations as the first target for the advance against the Soviet fortress and for the decisive blow in the "soft-belly" of the Soviet-Union. Yet, as the strength of a chain depends upon its weakest link, Ukraine may well determine the fate of a World Communist Empire, and serve in the future as the bulwark against centuries-long Russian expansionism and a strong wedge-like area of defence which would stabilize all this part of Europe.

Economically, Ukraine is one of the richest regions of Europe in agricultural and mineral resources. The chief agricultural products are wheat, rye, barley and sugar beets and livestock. The main mineral deposits are coal, iron and manganese. The range of resources makes possible not only industrialization, but fairly balanced economy.

Above all it is the political and moral potential of Ukraine, which will prove to be a decisive factor in the political reconstruction of Eastern Europe. Just as Soviet Union is the bulwark of the "Iron Curtain", so will a free and democratic Ukraine be one of the pillars of a new and better order in the world. In fact, no political structure in eastern Europe is possible without a free, democratic, united Ukraine, if this structure is to enjoy any degree of success. It is clear, that a free, democratic Ukraine will be able to safeguard the peace and to settle all problems of political, social, economic and cultural development of the Ukrainian better than the Soviet-Union could do it by ruling Ukraine by terror.

Following all these arguments, it would actually be in the interest of the United States to invent Ukraine, if there were none. But it is not necessary. Ukraine existed long before such an invention was necessary, exists now and will exist in the future. And it can be a most valuable ally behind the "Iron Curtain", if its possibilities are fully realized and exploited in the United States. The Western World would do well to recognize that in its struggle against aggressive, communist Russia, Ukraine will be called upon to play an important role. The sooner this realization comes, the better the chances are that Russia's drive to enslave and dominate the entire world will be broken and destroyed.

Today the American government has indisputable proof of the existence of the powerful Ukrainian Resistance Movement and its Ukrainian Insurgent Army (UPA), which has not laid down its arms against the Soviet aggressor. It is the great Achilles' heel of the Soviet Empire. The UPA, as the Ukrainian Insurgent Army is commonly known throughout Europe, is not only a symbol of the Ukrainian people but it is a rallying force of all anti-Soviet forces behind the "Iron Curtain". Its deeds are continually felt by the Russian totalitarians and their "quislings" in Ukraine, Poland, Czechoslovakia etc...

Dr. Fejes, the communist prosecutor in the Bratislava trial, revealed that the UPA-men were waging a fight, not only against the present regimes of Soviet-Ukraine and Czechoslovakia, but against all the "people's democracies" in Eastern Europe. He declared that all the "friends and sympathizers of the Soviet-Union and of the Communist idea had suffered at the hands of UPA." This charge was reinforced in its significance by the testimony of members of the Soviet army, the MVD, the Polish army and the UB, as well as the Czech army and NS (security police). They all emphasised the "dangerousness" of the UPA as well as of the Ukrainian Resistance Movement as a whole.

www.ingramcontent.com/pod-product-compliance
Ingram Content Group UK Ltd.
Pitfield, Milton Keynes, MK11 3LW, UK
UKHW051525180426
11947UKWH00019B/1583